THE TREATY OF UNION 1689–1740

Iain Johnston

The front cover shows the Scottish crown jewels, known as the Honours of Scotland. They date from the fifteenth and sixteenth centuries and comprise a crown, a sword and a sceptre. They are on display at Edinburgh Castle. The insert image shows the Duke of Queensberry presenting the Act of Union to Queen Anne in 1707.

The author would like to thank Lindsay Glover, John and Susan Galloway, Terry Heaviside, Colin Page, May Sharp and Carrie Munro.

The Publishers would like to thank the following for permission to reproduce copyright material:

Source 1.2 © The City of Edinburgh Council. Licensor www.scran.ac.uk; Source 1.8 © National Trust for Scotland. Licensor www.scran.ac.uk; Source 1.10 © Dundee City Council – Arts and Heritage. Licensor www.scran.ac.uk; Source 1.11 © Mary Evans Picture Library 2008; Source 1.12 © The National Trust for Scotland. Licensor www.scran.ac.uk; Source 1.13 © Agent/Daily Mail/Rex Features; Source 1.14 © Gallo Images/Travel Ink/Getty Images; Source 1.19 © National Museums Scotland. Licensor www.scran.ac.uk; Source 1.20 © Glasgow Museums. Licensor www.scran.ac.uk; Source 1.21 © National Museums Scotland. Licensor www.scran.ac.uk; Source 1.22 © British Geological Survey/NERC. All rights reserved. Licensor www.scran.ac.uk; Source 1.23 The Martyr of the Solway, 1871 (oil on canvas) by Millais, Sir John Everett (1829–96) © Walker Art Gallery, National Museums Liverpool/The Bridgeman Art Library; Source 1.24 © National Library of Scotland. Licensor www.scran.ac.uk; Source 1.27 © Hulton Archive/Getty Images; Source 1.28 © David Gowans/Alamy; Source 1.31 © Glasgow University Library, Special Collections; Source 1.37 © Paul Armiger; Source 1.42 © The Art Archive/Museo del Prado Madrid/Album/Joseph Martin; Source 1.46 James Douglas, 2nd Duke of Queensberry by Godfrey Kneller, 1701–1705 © Crown copyright: UK Government Art Collection; Source 1.48 Detail of Edinburgh: Nine Views of the Old Town, In Canongate, Foot of West Port, Calton (detail) by Anonymous. © City of Edinburgh Museums and Art Galleries, Scotland/ The Bridgeman Art Library; © www.Scottishviewpoint.com; Source 1.50 © The British Library/Heritage-Images Source 1.51 © National Library of Scotland. Licensor www.scran.ac.uk; Source 1.52 © International Photobank/Alamy; Source 2.1 © Scottish National Portrait Gallery. Licensor www.scran.ac.uk; Source 2.10 © National Galleries of Scotland. Licensor www.scran.ac.uk; Source 2.14 James Douglas (1658–1712) 4th Duke of Hamilton, c.1705 (oil on canvas) by Medina, Sir John Baptist de (1659–1710); Private Collection/© Philip Mould Ltd, London/The Bridgeman Art Library; Source 2.15 © National Galleries of Scotland. Licensor www.scran.ac.uk; Source 2.19 © National Trust for Scotland. Licensor www.scran.ac.uk; Source 2.28 © Edinburgh University Library. Licensor www.scran.ac.uk; Source 2.30 © Saul Gardiner. Licensor www.scran.ac.uk; Source 3.15 © Mary Evans Picture Library 2008; Source 3.16 © Royal Commission on the Ancient and Historical Monuments of Scotland. Licensor www.scran.ac.uk; Source 3.17 © Edinburgh City Libraries. Licensor www.scran.ac.uk; Source 3.18 © National Archives of Scotland. Licensor www.scran.ac.uk; Source 3.19 © Royal Commission on the Ancient and Historical Monuments of Scotland. Licensor www.scran.ac.uk; Source 3.20 © Crown Copyright reproduced courtesy of Historic Scotland. Licensor www.scran.ac.uk; Source 3.21 © Crown Copyright reproduced courtesy of Historic Scotland. Licensor www.scran.ac.uk; Source 4.1 King George I (oil on canvas) by Kneller, Sir Godfrey (1646–1723) © The Crown Estate/The Bridgeman Art Library; Source 4.11 © The Print Collector/Alamy; Source 4.15 © Dianne Sutherland. Licensor www.scran.ac.uk; Source 4.17 © James Gardiner. Licensor www.scran.ac.uk; Source 4.18 © National Galleries of Scotland. Licensor www.scran.ac.uk; Source 4.20 © Colin J M Martin. Licensor www.scran.ac.uk; Source 4.21 © Edinburgh City Libraries. Licensor www.scran.ac.uk; Source 4.26 © The Art Archive; Source 4.27 © Nick Haynes. Licensor www.scran.ac.uk; Source 4.28 © Royal Commission on the Ancient and Historical Monuments of Scotland; A/28612/cn. Licensor www.scran.ac.uk; Source 4.29 © David Tipling/Robert Harding World Imagery/Getty Images; Source 4.30 © Scottish Life Archive. Licensor www.scran.ac.uk; Source 4.31 © Gaidheil Alba/National Museums of Scotland. Licensor www.scran.ac.uk; Source 4.34 © University of Strathclyde. Licensor www.scran.ac.uk; Source 5.11 © Iain Green.

Acknowledgements

Every effort has been made to trace all copyright holders, but if any have been inadvertently overlooked the Publishers will be pleased to make the necessary arrangements at the first opportunity.

Although every effort has been made to ensure that website addresses are correct at time of going to press, Hodder Gibson cannot be held responsible for the content of any website mentioned in this book. It is sometimes possible to find a relocated web page by typing in the address of the home page for a website in the URL window of your browser.

Hachette's policy is to use papers that are natural, renewable and recyclable products and made from wood grown in sustainable forests. The logging and manufacturing processes are expected to conform to the environmental regulations of the country of origin.

Orders: please contact Bookpoint Ltd, 130 Milton Park, Abingdon, Oxon OX14 4SB. Telephone: (44) 01235 827720. Fax: (44) 01235 400454. Lines are open 9.00 – 5.00, Monday to Saturday, with a 24-hour message answering service. Visit our website at www.hoddereducation.co.uk. Hodder Gibson can be contacted direct on: Tel: 0141 848 1609; Fax: 0141 889 6315; email: hoddergibson@hodder.co.uk

© Iain Johnston 2010
First published in 2010 by
Hodder Gibson, an imprint of Hodder Education,
An Hachette UK Company,
2a Christie Street
Paisley PA1 1NB

Impression number   5 4 3 2 1
Year   2012 2011 2010

All rights reserved. Apart from any use permitted under UK copyright law, no part of this publication may be reproduced or transmitted in any form or by any means, electronic or mechanical, including photocopying and recording, or held within any information storage and retrieval system, without permission in writing from the publisher or under licence from the Copyright Licensing Agency Limited. Further details of such licences (for reprographic reproduction) may be obtained from the Copyright Licensing Agency Limited, Saffron House, 6–10 Kirby Street, London EC1N 8TS.

Cover photo © Scottish Viewpoint/Alamy; Mary Evans Picture Library (insert)
Illustrations by Jeff Edwards
Typeset in Sabon 10pt by Pantek Arts Ltd
Printed in Italy

A catalogue record for this title is available from the British Library

ISBN-13: 978 0340 98756 8

Contents

Introduction iv

1. The Background to the Union and the Worsening Relationship with England 1689–1705 1
2. Arguments For and Against the Union 40
3. The Passing of the Treaty of Union 60
4. The Effects of the Union 79
5. Looking Back on the Union 106

Preparing for Paper 2 of the Higher History Exam 114

References 134

Bibliography 138

Timeline 141

Places in Scotland Mentioned in This Book 143

Index 144

Introduction

Who is this book for?

The books in this series are for students following the new Scottish Higher History Course. Each book in this series covers all you need to know about one of the most popular topics in Paper 2 of the newly revised Scottish Higher History course. The entire syllabus is covered so you can be sure all your needs will be met.

What is in this book?

From 2011, Paper 2 of your Higher History exam is completely different from any earlier Higher History exam paper. There are five completely new Scottish-based topics. These topics are:

- The Wars of Independence 1286–1328

- The Age of the Reformation 1542–1603

- The Treaty of Union 1689–1740

- Migration and Empire 1830–1939

- The Impact of the Great War 1914–1928

Each topic is divided into six issues. Check out the Arrangments document on the SQA website at: www.sqa.org.uk. There you will find detailed descriptions of the content that is in each and every topic in Paper 2.

The first section you will see is called 'Background'. The last section is called 'Perspective'. Neither of those sections will have any questions asked about them. They are NOT examined. That leaves four main issues, and each one of those issues has a question linked to it.

What do I have to do to be successful?

In Paper 2, all assessments will be in the form of questions based on primary or secondary sources and in this series there is full coverage of all four types of questions you will meet. You will have five sources to use and four questions to answer.

You will have 1 hour and 25 minutes to do that. That means you will have about 20 minutes to deal with each question so your answers must be well structured and well developed. Put simply, that means you must do three things in each question:

1 You must do what you are asked to do.
2 You must refer to information in the source.
3 You must also include your own relevant recalled knowledge.

Topic: The Treaty of Union 1689–1740	
Background	looks at the constitutional, social and religious situation in 1689 following the Revolution Settlement.
Issue 1	examines the causes of the worsening relationship with England, including the Navigation Acts, Darien Scheme, foreign wars and famine.
Issue 2	looks at the arguments for and against Union with England, including religious and economic considerations, the accessibility of colonies, the issue of Scottish identity and the varied attitudes within Scotland towards Union.
Issue 3	explores the reasons why the Treaty of Union was passed, including changing English attitudes, the role of Commissioners and the negotiation process.
Issue 4	looks at the impact of Union in Scotland, economically and politically.
Perspective	considers the role that the Union played in the development of Scottish identity.

In the final chapter of this book there are not only examples of questions, but also full explanations of what makes good and not so good answers to the differing questions. Each type of question has its own particular process you must use to answer it successfully. In this section you will also find clear explanations of how marks are allocated so that your answers can be structured to gain the best possible score.

What types of questions will I be asked?

There are FOUR different types of question. Each type will be in your exam paper.

Question Type 1 is a source evaluation question worth 5 marks. It will usually be identified with a question asking, 'How useful is Source A as evidence…'

In this type of question you are being asked to judge how good the source is as a piece of historical evidence.

Question Type 2 is a comparison question worth 5 marks. You will be asked to compare two points of view overall and in detail. The question MIGHT NOT use the word 'compare' in the question.

The wording of the question could be something like 'To what extent does Source B agree with Source C about…'

Question Type 3 is a 'How far' question and is worth 10 marks. This question is to test your knowledge on one specific part of an issue, called a sub-issue. You can find all the sub-issues in the column called 'detailed descriptors' on the SQA syllabus website at: www.sqa.org.uk.

Question Type 4 is a 'How fully' question and is worth 10 marks. This question is to test your knowledge of a whole issue. Remember there are four issues in the syllabus on which you can be examined.

To summarise...

This book will help you to be successful in Paper 2 of the Scottish Higher History course. To be successful you must recognise the type of question you are being asked, follow the process for answering that type of question and also show off your own knowledge of the topic.

Beware: The four question types explained here **WILL** appear in the exam paper every year but will **NOT** appear in the same order every year. You will need to stay alert and be ready for them in any order.

1 The Background to the Union and the Worsening Relationship with England 1689–1705

The Succession and the Glorious Revolution 1688–89

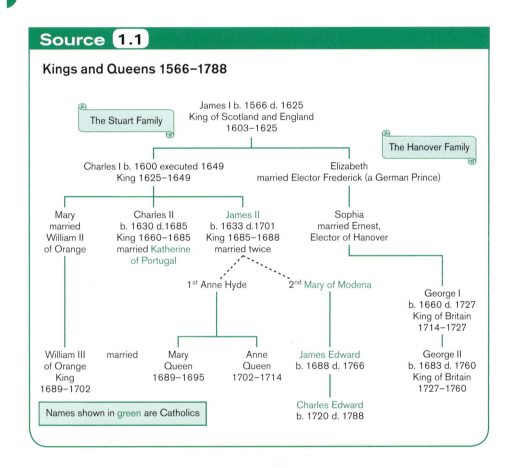

Source 1.1

Kings and Queens 1566–1788

Names shown in green are Catholics

William of Orange invaded England in November 1688. He was a Protestant Dutch prince from the House of Orange – this explains his name. William wore a harness. This was made of leather straps to support his humped back. He was very thin, short, coughed a lot because of asthma, possessed a hooked nose and had a scarred face because of smallpox. Some people thought that he had sinned because his wife Mary was also his niece. William's ambitions and policies caused difficulties in Anglo–Scottish relations.

William had no interest in Scotland and never visited. In the 1690s, Scotland attempted to establish a colony at Darien, near present-day Panama in central America. It failed and many Scots held William directly responsible. His reputation took another blow when his Scottish Government planned the Massacre of Glencoe in 1692. Famine also occurred in the 1690s. Opponents of William in Scotland called this period 'King William's seven ill years'. Scotland's experience of William's reign was far from the Glorious Revolution myth that was created by his propaganda.

William's propaganda said that he had come to Britain to defend Protestantism. This was not the whole story. William was actually quite tolerant of other religions. William's first concern was to protect his homeland. This is what we now call the Netherlands but in William's time it was known as the United Provinces. It was constantly under threat of attack from France, which was ruled by Louis XIV at that time. To defend the Netherlands, William was prepared to enter into alliances with both Protestant and Catholic monarchs. William did not hate Catholics. William did, however, need control of the English army and navy to use against the French. This is why he invaded England. William also needed to make sure that Scotland did not pose any problems during his war in Europe against Louis XIV's France. To this end, William agreed to a Presbyterian settlement of the Scottish Church in 1690. In return, the Scottish Parliament granted William 28 months of funding for his war against the French.

Source 1.2

The Orange Lodge is an organisation which promotes Protestant beliefs. Roman Catholics are excluded from membership

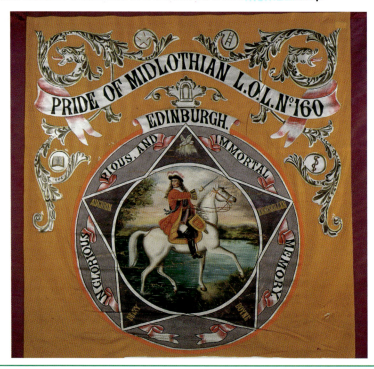

Source 1.2 shows a modern-day Orange Lodge banner from Scotland. It celebrates the triumph of William and Protestantism in 1688–89. William appears attractive and the revolution is considered 'Glorious'. As a historian, you need to decide whether this banner presents a balanced account. William was brave, but he was not a great military commander and did not ride a white horse into any battle.

The Scottish Parliament had to decide whether to accept William and his wife Mary as the new King and Queen. Protestants had become increasingly concerned about James VII of Scotland (also known as James II of England) because both he and his wife Mary were Roman Catholics. In England, James had replaced key post-holders in the army, government and church with Catholics. In Scotland, he allowed Catholics freedom of worship and membership of the Privy Council, which had a key role in government. He also established a Catholic chapel, school and printing press at Holyrood in Edinburgh.

You will learn on pages 14–19 that Presbyterians (Scottish Protestants) were persecuted in the 1680s by James VII. Protestants feared for their religion, parliament, laws, liberties and jobs. They thought that James may attack these in the same manner as the Catholic King Louis XIV of France had done in his own country. Louis' style of kingship was called Catholic absolutism. The birth of a son to James and his wife on 10 June 1688 seemed to threaten a long period of Catholic absolutism in Britain.

The Scottish Parliament received two letters from William and James each asking for support.

On 11 April 1689, the Scottish Parliament produced the Claim of Right. This document offered the crown to William and Mary on condition that they agreed to remedy the abuses of James VII's reign. The document stated that James had 'forfeited' the crown as a result of his behaviour.

The Claim of Right 1689 was accompanied by another document called the Articles of Grievance. This aimed to end the monarch's control over the Scottish Parliament, by making what could be discussed completely free. William and Mary reluctantly accepted both

Source 1.3

William's letter to the Scottish Parliament wrote about the importance of:

'securing the Protestant religion, the ancient laws and liberties of that kingdom… and… peace'.

Source 1.4

James' letter to the Scottish Parliament was more menacing:

'… we will punish with… our laws all such as shall stand out in rebellion against us and our authority.'

documents. The Scottish Parliament had imposed greater limitations upon royal power compared to the English settlement. Trying to limit the monarch's power was to become one of many problems in Anglo–Scottish relations under Queen Anne.

William's letter to the Scottish Parliament had expressed his hope for a more complete Union between Scotland and England. This was seen as a means to ensuring a peaceful Britain. This would have allowed William to fight his continental war (against Louis XIV's France) without fear of a backdoor military invasion from Scotland. What William got instead was his nightmare: a Jacobite rebellion.

Activities

1. Work in pairs. Make two columns with one headed 'Reasons For' and the other 'Reasons Against' accepting William and Mary as the new monarchs. Use the information on pages 1–4 to complete your columns.
2. Would you have accepted William and Mary as the new monarchs in 1689? What would have been the reasons for your decision?

The Jacobite Rising of 1689

The Latin for James is Jacobus and so the supporters of James VII were called Jacobites. James was the seventh King of Scotland with that name, but only the second in England – this is why he is known as both James II and James VII. In 1689, the Jacobites rebelled against the new monarchs William of Orange and his wife Mary. They wanted to put James VII back on to the British throne.

The Highland Gaelic poet Iain Lom (John MacDonald of Keppoch, c. 1624–1710) was a Jacobite. He wrote the poem in Source 1.5 which criticised William for seizing the throne and marrying his niece. Iain Lom was so angry that he hoped William would have a violent death, have no children and go to Hell!

Source 1.5

Jacobite Iain Lom's poem criticising William:

'This ungodly Prince of Orange! Although you would be drowned it is not such a death as I would wish for you, but to see you dragged between horses with thousands watching you, till you leap up in the air in small pieces with no offspring to gather round your elbow from the fruits of evil Mary's womb.'

Source 1.6 shows a map of Jacobite support in 1689. It was mainly clans from the Central Highlands who supported the 1689 Jacobite rising.

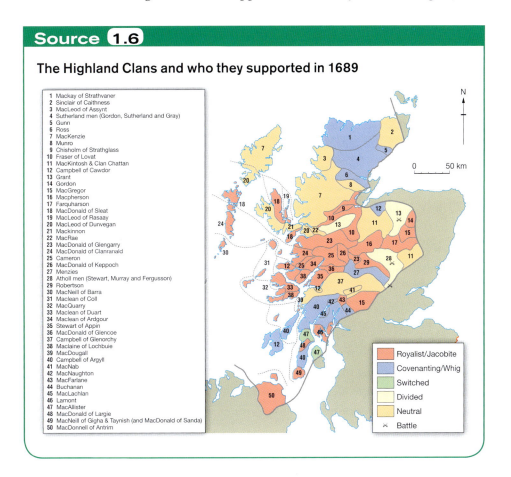

The supporters of William of Orange and Mary called their seizure of the British throne in 1688–89 the Glorious Revolution. In England, there was no fighting or blood spilled. In Scotland, James Graham, Viscount Claverhouse, led the first Jacobite rebellion.

Source 1.7 is written by the modern historian B. Lenman. He believes that loyalty to James VII was more important than hatred of the Campbells in explaining Highland clan support for the Jacobites in 1689.

Source 1.7

B. Lenman writes:

'The most important single motive in his [Claverhouse's] ranks seems to have been straightforward loyalty to the dynasty [James VII & II]. It is fashionable to argue that many Highlanders fought for the Stuarts primarily because they hated the Campbells, at once the staunchest [strongest] of Whigs [Government supporters], and the most aggressive of clans. In fact the latter title could be hotly contested by the MacKenzies or Gordons, and the hostility of many Jacobites to the Campbells can be grossly exaggerated'.

On 27 July 1689 the Jacobite army faced King William's government army at the narrow pass of Killiecrankie. The Jacobites were approximately 2000–2500 strong and the government army had about 4000 men. Both armies had to wait two hours before the battle could start because the sun was in their eyes! The Jacobites occupied the high ground through the pass and attacked their enemy using the terrifying 'Highland Charge' down a hillside. The government army was inexperienced: they only fired their guns once and then fled. The battle was over in minutes.

The modern painting in Source 1.8 tries to show what happened at the Battle of Killiecrankie. Government casualties amounted to about 1200 men either killed or wounded. The Jacobites lost approximately half that number.

Source 1.8

The Battle of Killiecrankie, 1689. Can you see the Highland Charge taking place?

Source 1.9 is an eye-witness account of the Battle of Killiecrankie from a letter written to James VII. It describes how the Highland Charge by the clansmen broke through the inexperienced and too thinly spread government line. It was a Jacobite victory.

Source 1.10

A nineteenth century painter's view of a Highlander with sword and targe

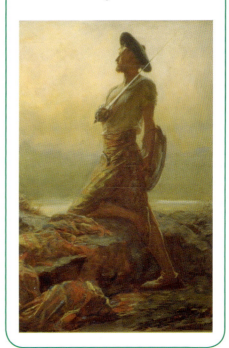

Source 1.9

Eye-witness account of the Battle of Killiecrankie:

'The Highlanders suffered their [government] fire with courage – then, when nearer them, delivered their own, and with sword and targe [a light shield] rapidly broke through their line and fell upon their flanks and rear, so that, in a moment whole intervals of [the government] front gave way and fled.'

Unfortunately for the Jacobites, their leader Viscount Claverhouse died from a stray musket ball at Killiecrankie. This dramatic moment is captured by a modern artist in Source 1.11. How accurate do you think this drawing is? Claverhouse's metal breastplate is on display in Blair Castle. The 4th Duke of Atholl (1755–1830) had a hole bored into it so that the breastplate would have a more dramatic effect on visitors!

Source 1.11

Claverhouse's Last Charge

Source 1.12

The Soldier's Leap

Source 1.12 is a photograph of the River Garry close to where the Battle of Killiecrankie took place. It shows the point where a government soldier, Donald MacBean, escaped. He leapt across the river from the rocks on one side to the rocks on the other side. The spot is called 'The Soldier's Leap'.

Without their leader, the Jacobite army was defeated at the Haughs of Cromdale on 1 May 1690. They had earlier been forced to withdraw from Dunkeld on 21 August 1689 by a government force. This was the end of the first Jacobite rebellion.

Jacobitism in 1689 was limited in the extent of the threat posed. Jacobite forces led by James VII in Ireland were defeated at the Battle of the Boyne on 12 July 1690. On 3 October 1691 the Treaty of Limerick recognised the English conquest of Ireland. However, Jacobitism, especially in the Highlands, was a threat which King William could well do without. William was involved in the Nine Years' War (1689–1697) against his bitter enemy: France. William's Scottish Government knew that the Jacobite threat had to be kept quiet. This helps to explain why the Massacre of Glencoe, in 1692, was ordered.

Activities

1. Write out 10 questions about the Jacobite rebellion in 1689. You must be able to find the answers on pages 4–9.
2. Test these questions on your fellow class members.
   - Work in pairs.
   - One person asks their questions and their partner gives their answers.
   - Then change over so that your partner is asking the questions.
   - You are only allowed one minute to ask and receive answers to your questions.
   - Change partners and keep a record of your own score.

The Massacre of Glencoe 1692

In the early morning of 13 February 1692, Captain Robert Campbell of Glenlyon and his 60 soldiers murdered 38 MacDonalds who lived in Glencoe. The rest of the clan, approximately 600 people, fled into a blizzard. The soldiers had spent the previous 12 days living, eating, sleeping, storytelling and playing cards with the MacDonalds in their homes. The MacDonalds believed that the soldiers had come to collect

taxes and because there was no room available at Inverlochy Fort (Fort William) they had come to stay with them. The events of that morning became known as 'the Massacre of Glencoe'.

Source 1.13

A painting of the Massacre of Glencoe by James Hamilton (1853–1894). How can you tell the painter is sympathetic to the MacDonalds?

It seems highly probable that only 38 MacDonalds died because the whole affair was mishandled. Not all the escape routes had been secured and the soldiers used easily-heard musket fire. There are also stories about advance warnings being given by individual soldiers, while others appear to have had no stomach for the whole affair. One story tells of how a mother and baby, to whom she was singing a lullaby, were found hiding in the snow by a soldier. The soldier shot their dog and claimed that the blood came from MacDonald survivors.

On the other hand, some soldiers seem to have enjoyed their orders. MacIain was the Clan Chief of the Glencoe MacDonalds and was shot in the back and head, while two soldiers used their teeth to pull the rings from his wife's fingers. She was stripped naked and fled into the snow only to die the next day of her injuries. Another story tells of how one soldier stabbed a young boy in the back as he grabbed around Captain Glenlyon's knees and begged for mercy. Eight MacDonald men were shot at through the windows in one house. One injured MacDonald asked to be taken outside to be shot. He threw his tartan plaid over the firing squad and escaped to tell his story. Other survivors escaped by the back door.

In the 1960s a film about the Massacre was produced that suggested it was part of a long-standing feud (dispute) between the MacDonald and Campbell clans. This was also the view of the Gaelic poet Iain Lom (John MacDonald of Keppoch). Even today, if you visit the Clachaig Inn in Glencoe you will see the inscription above the door 'No Campbells'.

A letter from the Earl of Stair states that the two most powerful Campbell Chiefs, the Earls of Breadalbane and Argyll, were both fully aware of the planned massacre. They offered to prevent the MacDonalds of Glencoe having an escape route through their Campbell lands. Breadalbane had lost cattle, stolen by the MacDonalds of Glencoe.

Source 1.14

The memorial to the Massacre of Glencoe, situated in the village of Glencoe

The Massacre of Glencoe, however, was not just about Campbell–MacDonald rivalry. Glenlyon's regiment, who carried out the massacre, was not full of Campbells. It contained Lowlanders and one English sergeant. The real importance of the Massacre of Glencoe lay in what it said about King William's Scottish Government and the King's attitude to Scottish affairs.

Why did the Massacre take place?

The Jacobite Rising of 1689 had shown William the danger posed by the Highland clans loyal to the exiled James VII. All clans were required to sign and swear allegiance to King William by 1 January 1692. Unfortunately, the clan chief MacIain of Glencoe only found out on 30 December 1691 that James VII had granted permission to do so. MacIain set off through the snow for Fort William that same day but, on reaching Inverlochy Fort, was informed by Colonel Hill that the oath could only be taken at Inveraray, some 74 miles away.

Too late!

MacIain arrived at Inveraray on 2 January 1692. Unfortunately, the local sheriff Colin Campbell of Ardkinglas was still away celebrating the New Year. He only returned on 5 January 1692. After much persuasion, he eventually accepted MacIain's late oath of allegiance. Colin Campbell wrote to government officials in Edinburgh confirming that MacIain had taken the oath. MacIain assumed that everything was fine when he received

a letter from Colonel Hill stating that he was now under the protection of the garrison at Inverlochy in Fort William.

MacIain's name, however, was removed from the list of those who had taken the oath by government officers in Edinburgh. These officers were Campbell lawyers. Powerful individuals within William's Scottish Government now advanced their own interests. Sir John Dalrymple (Earl of Stair) saw the opportunity to demonstrate to King William that he could control Scotland for him, by making an example of the MacDonalds of Glencoe.

Dalrymple was a Lowlander. He hated the highlanders and did not understand their clan society or the Gaelic language. Dalrymple's involvement in the Massacre is the reason for the nine of diamonds in a pack of playing cards being called 'the curse of Scotland' – the card resembles the Dalrymple coat of arms.

Source 1.16 is from the King's instructions to Colonel Hill at Inverlochy Fort, dated 16 January 1692. The instructions were probably written by the Earl of Stair. As well as MacIain, the Clan Chief of the MacDonalds from Glengarry had also not taken the oath to King William in time. The MacDonalds were more powerful, however, and too difficult to act against given the bad weather.

King William's signature appeared twice on the 16 January order but the official Report of the Glencoe Enquiry 1695 (Source 1.17) offered a very different interpretation as to what King William had intended to happen to the Glencoe MacDonalds. It flatly denied that William had wanted violence used against them.

Source 1.15

Sir John Dalrymple wrote on 11 January 1692:

'Just now, my Lord Argyle tells me that Glencoe hath not taken the oaths, at which I rejoice, it's a great work of charity to be exact in rooting out that damnable sect, the worst in all the Highlands.'

Source 1.16

The King's instructions to Colonel Hill:

'We do allow you to receive the submission of Glengarry and those with him, upon their taking the oath of allegiance and delivering up the house of Invergarry, to be safe as to their lives, the house of Invergarry cannot probably be taken in this season of the year, with the artillery and provision you can bring there. If MacIain of Glencoe and that tribe can well be separated from the rest, it will be a proper vindication [use] of public Justice to extirpate [annihilate] that sect of thieves.'

King William's direct involvement in the Glencoe Massacre is not proven. There is, however, no doubt that the military high command in Scotland fully co-operated in carrying out the Massacre. Sir Thomas Livingstone, Commander of the government forces in Scotland, had written to Lieutenant Colonel Hamilton at Fort William on 23 January 1692 and instructed him to 'not trouble the government with prisoners' from Glencoe (Quoted in MacDonald, 1982).

The order (see Source 1.18) sent to Captain Robert Campbell of Glenlyon on 12 January 1692 was signed by Major Duncanson. Glenlyon had to carry out his orders or be kicked out of the army.

Captain Robert Campbell had no choice but to obey the order. He had large debts from a life of gambling and drunkenness. The instruction to commence at 5a.m. seems to have been changed from the original instruction of 7a.m. This was to ensure that Campbell of Glenlyon would be held responsible for the Massacre before the other main officers – Major Robert Duncanson, Captain Drummond and Lieutenant Colonel Hamilton – arrived from having secured the escape routes. The official enquiry in 1695 blamed the Earl of Stair and various military officers for the Massacre, but no one ever stood trial.

Source 1.17

The official Report of the Glencoe Enquiry 1695:

'That there was nothing in the King's Instructions to warrant the committing of the foresaid slaughter. He [William] ordered nothing concerning Glencoe and his tribe that if they could be separated from the rest it would be a proper vindication of the Public Justice to extirpate that sect of thieves unless they still refused his mercy by continuing in arms and refusing the allegiance. And even in that case they were only to be proceeded against in the way of public justice [legal means] and no other ways.'

Source 1.18

Order sent to Captain Robert Campbell of Glenlyon:

'Sir
You are hereby ordered to fall upon the rebels of the MacDonalds of Glencoe, and put all to the sword under 70. You are to have especial care, that the Old Fox [MacIain] and his sons do upon no account escape your hands; you are to secure all the avenues, that no man escape; this you are to put in execution at five a clock in the morning precisely. See that this be put in execution else you may expect to be treated as not true to the King or Government, nor a man fit to carry commission in the King's service.'

How did the Massacre help the Jacobites and harm the Government?

In the summer and autumn of 1690 a government force burned, murdered and raped its way through various parts of the Inner Hebrides. The numbers affected were probably greater than the events in Glencoe but this event did not achieve the same publicity. Rival clans had also committed extreme acts of brutality towards each other in their past. In 1577, in a cave on the Island of Eigg, 390 MacDonalds had been suffocated to death by a rival clan of MacLeods, who set fire to the only way in or out. The problem for King William was that the events of Glencoe became national and international news.

Captain Robert Campbell lost copies of his Glencoe orders, while drunk in Edinburgh, on his way to Flanders (Belgium). These orders were stolen and sent to France by Jacobites. By April 1692, the Glencoe Massacre was international news in the Paris Gazette. The Jacobite Charles Leslie also talked to soldiers who were present at the Glencoe Massacre and produced pamphlets about it. The Massacre of Glencoe was a public relations disaster for King William and his Scottish Government. It breathed new life into the Jacobite cause and allowed opponents of King William's Scottish Government to level criticism.

William, because of a lack of interest in Scottish affairs, had allowed his Scottish Government to commit treason against its own people. Under Scottish law, William's Scottish Government was guilty of 'slaughter under trust'. In the twenty-first century such an act would be considered as ethnic cleansing. This means deliberately planning and carrying out the murder of one group of people by another. This did nothing to help Anglo-Scottish relations because it demonstrated William's lack of real concern for Scottish affairs.

Activities

1. Work in pairs. Make a list of the following people: King William; the Earl of Stair; Sir James Dalrymple; the Earl of Argyll; the Earl of Breadalbane; the military high command in Scotland; Robert Campbell of Glenlyon; Robert Campbell of Glenlyon's regiment of soldiers; the Campbell lawyers in Edinburgh who were government officers. Allocate a percentage of the blame to each person in the list for the Massacre of Glencoe.
2. What are your reasons for each decision?
3. Compare your percentage blame list with the lists of other class members.

Religion

Scotland was deeply religious in this early modern period, but also brutal and intolerant. 'Thou shalt not suffer a witch to live' is an instruction found in the King James VI bible. In the Fife village of Pittenweem in 1704–5, the high court freed a number of women accused of witchcraft. The local minister led a mob that chased those released. One of the women, Janet Cornfoot, was caught and crushed under a door weighted with rocks on top. Witches could still be executed in Scotland until 1727.

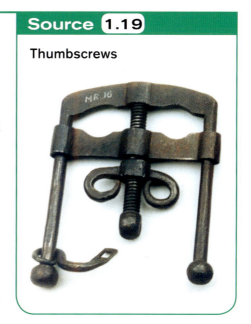

Source 1.19

Thumbscrews

Source 1.19 shows a set of thumbscrews. They were invented by Bishop Paterson in the 1680s as an instrument of torture.

An Edinburgh student, Thomas Aikenhead, was hanged in 1697 for claiming that Jesus had performed 'cheap magic tricks' rather than miracles, and for calling his followers (the Apostles) 'a company of silly witless fishermen'. (Herman, 2001.)

After the mid-sixteenth century Scotland was officially Presbyterian. This was Protestant, but in a church without bishops. Presbyterians believed in a church organisation with different types of governing bodies. These included kirk sessions, presbyteries, synods and a General Assembly.

Charles II reigned from 1660–1685. He reintroduced bishops to the Scottish church. He also claimed to be head of the church and demanded everyone accepted this by swearing an oath. This became known as the 1681 Test Act and it went against Scottish Presbyterian beliefs.

During James VII's reign (1685–89) tolerance for Catholics was attempted. Extreme Presbyterians, in particular from the south and west of Scotland, opposed this. They were known as Covenanters and believed that only Jesus Christ could be head of their church. These groups had a tradition of attending secret outdoor religious services in order to avoid persecution.

Source 1.20 is a nineteenth-century painting of a seventeenth-century Covenanters meeting. Covenanters took their name from the Presbyterians who had signed the National Covenant in 1638 against Charles I's religious changes. The painting shows a relaxed and well organised meeting, in nice evening weather. This was not always the case.

Source 1.20

The Covenanters' Preaching by Sir George Harvey c. 1830

In the 1680s, under Charles II and James VII, moderate and radical Presbyterians were persecuted, especially in the south-west of Scotland. This was known as 'the Killing Time'. The nineteenth-century writer Sir Walter Scott gave James Graham of Claverhouse, who led the 1689 Jacobite Rebellion, the nickname 'Bonnie Dundee'. To the Covenanters of the south-west he was known by a different name – 'Bluidy (Bloody) Clavers' – because of his brutal behaviour.

Source 1.21

The mask worn by Alexander Peden

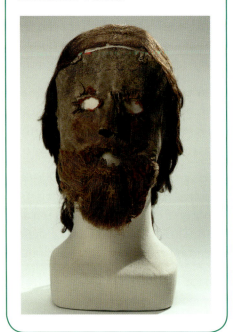

Source 1.21 shows a mask worn by Alexander Peden, a Covenanting minister in the south-west. He used it to hide his identity when he was not attending secret outdoor religious meetings. People thought that he possessed some terrible illness and so stayed away from him. He used a cave at Sorn in East Ayrshire as a hideout.

Source 1.22 is a photograph of the Bass Rock in the Firth of Forth. It was used to imprison Covenanters and moderate Presbyterians in the 1680s. Prisoners had to drink rainwater, snow and ice, suffered poor quality food for which they had to pay and enjoyed only limited time out of their cramped cells.

Source 1.22

The Bass Rock

Source 1.23

This modern painting shows Margaret Wilson, one of the two female Wigtown Martyrs

A martyr is someone who is prepared to die for what they believe in rather than give it up. The Wigtown Martyrs refused to take the 1681 oath recognising Charles II as head of the Scottish Church. They were tied to wooden poles on the local beach and drowned as the tide came in. One woman was tied further out so that the other woman had to watch!

Not all historians are convinced that the story of the Wigtown Martyrs is true. Other stories from the 1680s may also have question marks about their accuracy. Sir Robert Grierson is supposed to have captured the Covenanters in spike-filled wooden barrels and rolled them down the nearest hill. It is reckoned, however, that under the reigns of Charles II and James VII approximately 680 Covenanters were killed fighting, 498 murdered and 362 executed.

The extreme Presbyterians were also capable of savage acts. In May 1679 Archbishop Sharp's stagecoach was ambushed. He was slain with multiple stab wounds in front of his daughter. Source 1.24 is a broadsheet (a newssheet) from the time showing the event.

Source 1.24

What evidence can you find in the broadsheet to support the view that the murder of Archbishop Sharp was seen as an outrageous act?

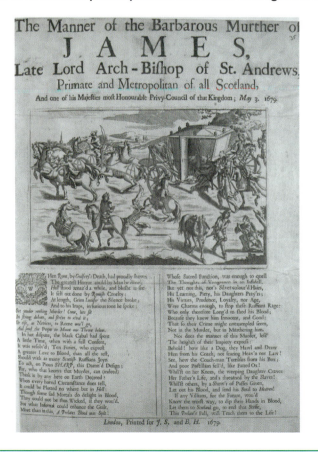

Religious beliefs and the experiences of the 1680s helped to shape attitudes towards King William of Orange, the Jacobites and a full incorporating union with England.

Extreme Presbyterians in the south-west opposed a full incorporating union because England had a church containing bishops. Extreme Presbyterians were also not willing to fight beside Catholic and Episcopalian Jacobite supporters. Episcopalians were Protestant but allowed bishops into their church and recognised the Catholic James VII as the rightful monarch.

Moderate Presbyterians would also not accept any degree of tolerance for Catholicism. Some supporters of the Union in 1707, or their close relatives, had personally suffered for their Presbyterian religious beliefs in the 1680s. The Reverend William Carstares had been tortured with thumbscrews and the Earl of Marchmont imprisoned on the Bass Rock. He fled to Holland after spending a month hiding in the pitch-dark cellar of a local church.

Unlike the extreme Covenanters, the moderate Presbyterians were prepared to consider a full union with England. The Scottish Parliament had approved a Presbyterian settlement of the Church in Scotland in 1690 and around 200 Episcopalian ministers were removed from their parishes. Moderate Presbyterians played a key role in supporting the Protestant William of Orange from 1688–89 and they wanted further guarantees for their religion if a full union with England was established.

In 1689, at the start of your period of study, concern about the future of Presbyterianism was a key issue. Presbyterians wanted to ensure that the treatment they experienced in the 1680s could never happen again. They viewed the Jacobites, who wanted to restore a Catholic monarch, with horror.

Activities

1. It is 1689 and you are a Presbyterian. Design a poster which clearly shows why a Catholic monarch should not be restored. You can draw on any of the experiences of Presbyterians described on pages 14–19 for ideas. You can use both visual images and writing. Remember, the central idea is the fear of persecution under a Catholic monarch.

2. Present your poster to the rest of the class and explain its content. The class should judge which poster and presentation would have been most effective in 1689. What will be your criteria for deciding this?

International Trade

By 1700, the major European powers had established empires across the globe.

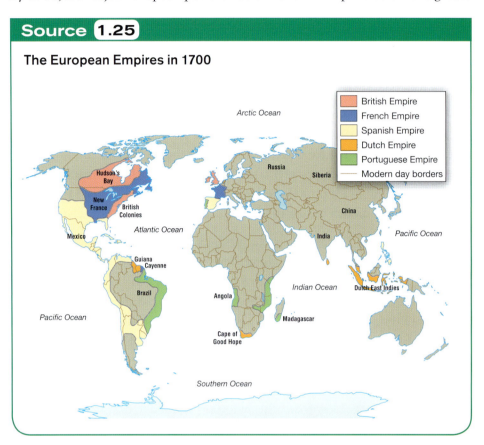

Source 1.25

The European Empires in 1700

It was an age of fierce European competition on both land and sea for the control of colonies. These were seen as the key to increasing trade and wealth. Historians refer to this period as an age of mercantilism. This means that the major European powers put taxes and restrictions on the trading and sale of goods by rival countries with any of their colonies. This happened increasingly after the 1690s. Although Scotland became part of the United Kingdom after 1603, with James VI becoming James I of England, she was not allowed access to England's North American colonies. Navigation maps from before 1707 called these colonies 'the English empire in America'.

A series of Navigation Acts passed by the English Parliament in the 1660s and 1670s, prevented Scotland from being able to trade with England's colonies. There were, however, large numbers of Scots who lived within the colonies of the 'English' empire. This Scottish presence within the Empire included Boston, New York, Philadelphia, New England, the Southern colonies of America trading in tobacco and sugar, and the Caribbean.

There is a district called Scotland on the Island of Barbados. Not only did these areas of Scottish influence trade with England's rivals, including the Dutch, French and Danes, they also ignored the Navigation Acts.

Source 1.26

Places in America with a large number of Scottish settlers and traders by 1700

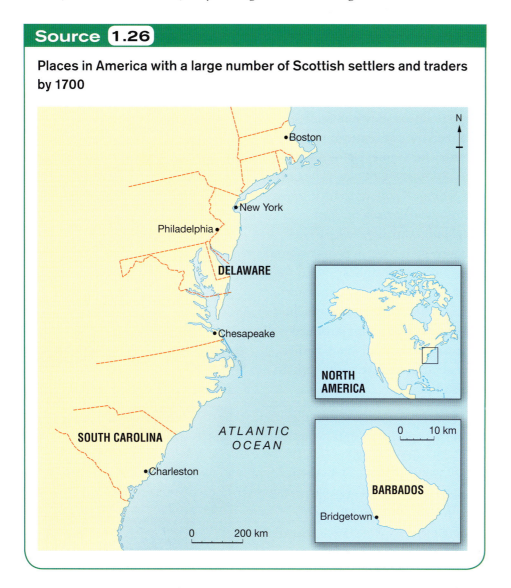

The Scots were able to bring their experience of 'tramping' from the Baltic trade and apply it to North America and the Caribbean. Tramping involved the transfer of goods between several ships using different ports. The Scots also forged documentation for illegal trade by their ships and bribed officials. It proved very difficult for the Navigation Acts to work. English officials in the American colonies started to complain about the Scots' success. The Scots' ability to ignore the Navigation Acts by the 1680s was considered a bigger problem than the pirates of the Caribbean.

Source 1.27 is a sketch from around 1700 of the pirate Captain William Kidd from Greenock in Scotland. He was arrested in Boston, America, and hanged for piracy in 1701. The cargo from Kidd's ship was never discovered. He was thought to have buried it on a Caribbean island. This story provided the inspiration for Robert Louis Stevenson's book *Treasure Island*.

A statue of Alexander Selkirk of Largo in Fife is shown in Source 1.28. Selkirk's adventures provided the story for Daniel Defoe's 1719 book *Robinson Crusoe – The Life and Strange Surprising Adventures of Robinson Crusoe of York (England), Mariner*. Selkirk was discovered, dressed in goatskins and struggling to remember how to speak English, on an uninhabited Pacific Island off the coast of Chile in 1709. He had been marooned there more than four years earlier after an argument with the captain of his ship.

The Scottish presence within the 'English' empire was significant by 1707. The attempts of James VII (1685–1688) to promote Scottish interests within the empire provided a further headache for English trading interests. He allowed Scottish participation in the English-controlled Royal Africa Company from the 1670s and the Hudson Bay Company in Canada from the 1680s.

After William of Orange seized the British throne in 1688–89, English interests within the empire were put first. William's English advisors and government ministers reminded him of the serious competition Scotland posed to English trade within the Empire. This helps to explain the opposition from both William and the

Source 1.27

Captain William Kidd

Source 1.28

Alexander Selkirk of Largo

English to the Scottish Darien Scheme. The outcome was more ill feeling in Anglo–Scottish relations.

> **Activities**
>
> 1 Design a crossword with a minimum of ten clues about Scotland's role in international trade by 1700. Remember to include clues for both across and down. Use the information on pages 20–23 to help you.
> 2 Swap crosswords with a partner and try to solve the clues.

The Darien Scheme 1695–1700

In the seventeenth century, colonies were seen as important for trade and wealth. The Scots tried to establish a colony in Central America, at Darien, in the 1690s. The idea was to control trade between the Atlantic and Pacific Oceans. The 50–60 mile route planned to use rivers and go overland. Some modern archaeologists believe that this was possible and a good idea. The route offered a short cut to ships because they would no longer have to sail around the dangerous seas at the tip of South America.

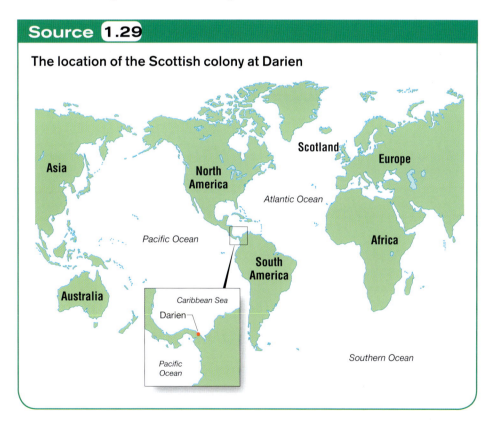

Source 1.29

The location of the Scottish colony at Darien

It took until the early twentieth century to build the modern-day Panama Canal in the same area as where Darien was planned. This would suggest that the idea of a colony at Darien in the 1690s was a difficult project to achieve. It was not helped by bad planning. The modern historian K. Brown, believes that 'the [Darien] enterprise was planned and executed with staggering incompetence' (Brown, 1993).

Source 1.30

William Paterson, a Scot, thought up the idea of Darien and was confident of its success:

'The time and expense of navigation to China, Japan and the Spice Islands, and the East Indies, will be reduced by more than half… Trade will increase trade, and money will make money…'

Source 1.31 shows a drawing made in the 1690s of the colony, which was named New Edinburgh, along with Fort St. Andrew. Sir John Dalrymple was a colonist at Darien. He described the mountains around Darien as one mile high. The colonists spent two months trying to build huts on nearby boggy ground before deciding Fort St. Andrew was a better idea.

Source 1.31

A drawing of the colony made in the 1690s

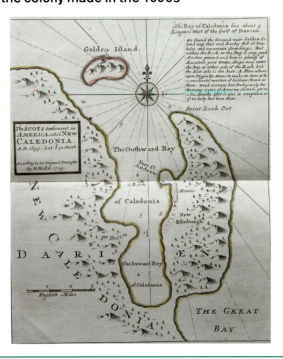

Darien was not suitable for Northern European settlement. The Spanish, who were used to considerably hotter weather than Scots, had attempted a settlement at Darien in 1501 but abandoned it by 1524. Darien has 200 inches of rainfall yearly because it is next to a tropical rainforest! The area is full of killer diseases including malaria, yellow fever, typhoid, cholera, dysentery and plague. There are also sand flies, poisonous snakes, plant diseases and even crop-eating crabs! The local Indians, the Tule, live on the islands offshore, rather than on the Darien mainland. Even today, few people live around Darien.

On 4 July 1698, 1200 colonists left Leith Harbour, near Edinburgh, and arrived at Darien on 2 November 1698. Forty-four colonists died during the voyage and 32 died shortly after arrival, including William Paterson's wife on 14 November. This was not a particularly bad casualty rate for journeys of the period but the voyage to Darien was poorly planned. There was not enough food taken onboard for the journey and the five Scottish ships only carried one small fishing net each! William Paterson had never actually visited Darien.

The diagram below shows the Company of Scotland's inexperience in trying to make Darien successful.

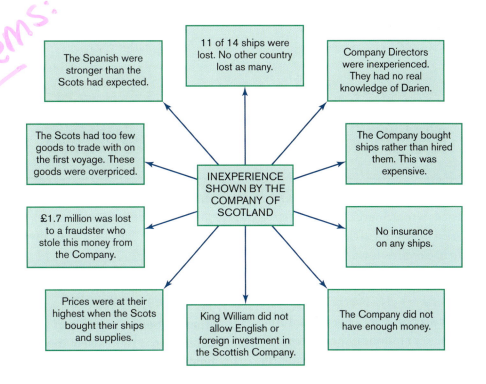

Both Paterson and the Company of Scotland Directors' decision to settle Darien may have been influenced by stories of gold, silver and timber told by two pirates! The London-based Scottish merchant Robert Douglas tried unsuccessfully to convince the company directors that a trading expedition to the East Indies made much more sense. There, the Dutch planned their colonies very carefully. They used engineers to plan and build their settlements and artists to draw pictures of what they looked like. These pictures were used to attract investment. The Scots did not even bother to find out whether Darien was suitable for settlement!

The settlement at Darien was basic, as the artist's impression in Source 1.32 shows. Nothing remains today, apart from one marked stone with Fort St. Andrew scratched on it. The rest of the area is covered in jungle.

Source 1.32

The settlement at Darien

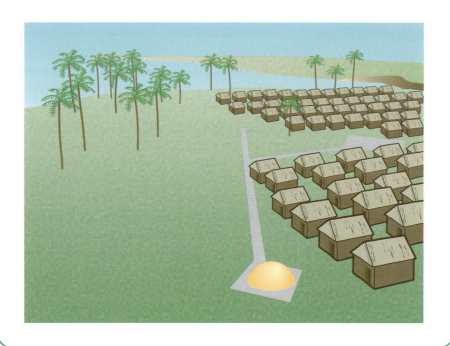

Captain Pennecuik, who was commander of the Scottish ships that arrived at Darien, wrote Source 1.33 on his arrival. He failed to realise that the Bay of Darien was impossible to leave against a northerly wind! The wind blew any ship backwards towards the shore.

The Scots' trading goods taken to Darien were also overpriced by about 40 per cent. This did nothing for the reputation of the Scottish colony. By spring 1699, the Scottish settlers were suffering severe food shortages. Roger Oswald was one of the Darien colonists. He recorded that they were surviving on less than a pound of mouldy flour a week and that the leadership was divided (see Source 1.34).

Source 1.33

Captain Pennecuik wrote:

'This Harbour is capable of containing a 1000 sail of the best ships in the world. And without great trouble wharfs [landing areas] may be run out, to which ships of the greatest burden [size] may unload.'

Source 1.35 is from a pamphlet from the 1690s. It records with disbelief that the Scottish colony at Darien was in the heart of the Spanish empire in the Americas. The Spanish used Carthagena as a port from which to ship

Source 1.34

Roger Oswald reported:

'When boiled with a little water, without anything else, big maggots and worms must be skimmed off the top. In short, a man might easily have destroyed his whole week's ration in one day. Yet for all this short allowance, every man daily turned out to work by daylight, whether with the hatchet, or wheelbarrow, pick-axe, shovel, fore-hammer or any other instrument and so continued until 12 o'clock, and at 2 again and stayed till night, sometimes working all day in water at the trenches. My shoulders have been so wore with carrying burdens that the skin has come off them and grew full of boils. If a man were sick and obliged to stay within, no victuals [food] for him that day. Our Councillors [were] divided into factions [and] we were like so many skeletons.'

gold and silver from their colonies back to Spain. They were not about to let the Scottish settlement be established as a rival.

Unfortunately, King William's foreign policy at that time made it important for him to remain on good terms with the Spanish. English officials in the Netherlands and Hamburg (Germany) prevented foreign investment in the Darien Scheme. English merchants and the English colonies, including Jamaica, Barbados and New York, were all forbidden by William to offer any assistance to the Scots at Darien. When the Scots at Darien learned about this in May 1699, they decided to abandon the colony. Only one ship out of the original five made it back to Scotland.

Source 1.35

A pamphlet from the 1690s:

'... the Company [of Scotland] had settled their colony in the very bosom and centre of the three chief cities of the Spanish–Indies… Carthagena, Portobello, and Panama, the first being 45 Leagues, [135 miles] and the other two not above 30 [60 miles] distant from the colony.'

Poor communication meant that two relief ships arrived at Darien in August 1699 only to find the colony deserted. One accidentally burned on arrival at Darien and the other went to Jamaica. The second Darien expedition of four ships set sail from the Clyde on 18 August 1699. They did not know that Darien had been abandoned. These colonists did no better than those in the first expedition. 160 died during the voyage because of unclean water and rotten food. This was twice the death rate on the first expedition.

The second expedition arrived at Darien on 30 November 1699. On 31 March 1700, the colonists surrendered to the Spanish after they had attacked the settlement. One account records that the Scots were too weak to take their ships out of harbour and they had to be towed out of the Bay of Caledonia by the Spanish. Two ships were sunk in a hurricane, one was shipwrecked and the other surrendered to the Spanish at Carthagena in April 1700.

Source 1.37 shows a photograph of actors from a 2003 television programme about Darien. This programme tried to put a more positive spin on the whole Darien affair. It argued that the Scots short-lived presence in Darien was popular with the native people because the Scots treated them fairly, started the basis of Panama's trading success and introduced democracy. This was unlike the Spanish who treated the natives as 'slave labour and inferior pests who could be ethnically cleansed'.

Source 1.36

Reverend Francis Borland, shortly after arriving at Darien on 30 November 1699, wrote:

'Darien is… unwholesome and contagious… Thou devourest men and eatest up thy inhabitants… What with bad water, salt spoiled provisions, and absence of medicines, the fort was indeed like an hospital of sick and dying men.'
[Borland also complained about drunkenness and swearing.]

Source 1.37

BBC production (2003) *Darien: Disaster in Paradise*

William of Orange had supported the Company of Scotland at the start. It was granted very generous trading terms. This may have been because of the bad publicity for both William and his Scottish Government after the Massacre of Glencoe in 1692. William did, however, receive an address from the Commons and Lords in England on 17 December 1695 protesting about 'the great prejudice, inconvenience and mischief' threatened to English trade by the Company of Scotland.

King William wrote Source 1.38. It shows a lack of interest in Scotland because William was prepared to withdraw all support for the colony at Darien. He thought that the Act of the Scottish Parliament, which established the Company of Scotland, should never have been allowed.

> **Source 1.38**
>
> **King William stated:**
>
> 'I have been ill-served in Scotland, but hope some remedies may be found to prevent the inconveniences which may arise from this Act.'

William could not afford to have his English Parliament refuse funding for his fight against Louis XIV in the Nine Years' War 1688–1697 because they were angry at the Darien Scheme. He also needed to keep the Spanish on good terms and avoid a war with them at the same time. This explains why the Scottish colony at Darien, in the heart of the Spanish empire in the Americas, could be sacrificed. It is possible that a Scottish settlement at Darien was also thought to be too dangerous because it may have encouraged nearby English colonies in America to break away and become independent.

The Scottish economy seemed to be in a bad way in the 1690s. The failure of the Darien Scheme to bring about economic recovery resulted in a mood of Anglophobia (an anti-English attitude) in Scotland. This was accompanied by a desire for compensation because a large number of Scots had invested money in the Company of Scotland and lost everything. King William's actions to prevent trading and his initial support for the Scottish settlement at Darien were resented and criticised.

Activities

1. Write the heading 'The Darien Scheme 1695–1700'. Beneath your heading divide the page into three columns. Title one column 'William', the second 'Planning' and the final column 'Darien the Place'.

   In each column list at least six facts for each topic which would help to explain why the Darien Scheme failed. Shade each column a different light colour (avoid heavy marker pens) to help differentiate them.

The Domestic Economy in the 1690s

In the last third of the seventeenth century a 'Little Ice Age' happened. It provided the most severe weather of the previous 10,000 years. It is estimated that perhaps a third of the population of Finland died, while famine struck Norway and Scotland in the 1690s. The effects upon some areas may have been worse than the dreadful Black Death of the Middle Ages.

The Little Ice Age may have resulted from a number of massive volcanic eruptions, including Hekla in Iceland (1693) and Serua (1693) and Aboina (1694), both in Indonesia. It is thought that sunlight was blocked by the ash that was pushed out into the atmosphere when the volcanoes erupted. The result was wetter and colder weather. Between 1693 and 1700 there were harvest failures in seven out of eight years and thousands of animals died. Stories were passed down from this time about men dropping dead with grass and raw flesh in their mouths!

Source 1.39

Sir Robert Sibbald's pamphlet in the 1690s advised the starving to eat herbs and even cat flesh to stay alive:

'When the bad seasons these several years past, hath made so much scarcity and so great a dearth [crop failure], that for want, some die by the way-side, some drop down on the streets, the poor sucking babs [babies] are starving for want of milk, which the empty breasts of their mothers cannot furnish them: Every one may see death in the face of the poor, that abound every where; the thinness of their visage [face], their ghostly looks, their feebleness, their agues [fevers] and their fluxes [sicknesses] threaten them with sudden death; if care be not taken of them.'

In Source 1.40, the Reverend Patrick Walker believed the famine to have been a judgment delivered by God for sinfulness. This included doing work on a Sunday and sex outside marriage. Jacobites thought differently. They thought the 1690s to have been God's judgement for accepting William as King.

Source 1.40

Reverend Patrick Walker recorded:

'These unheard-of judgments continued for seven years. Summers and winters were so cold and barren that the cattle, flying fowls and insects all decayed. Our harvests did not take place in ordinary months, [sometimes] in November. Many died or lost the use of their feet and hands, working in frost and snow. Meal [grain ground to powder for bread] became so scarce that it was expensive and many could not get it. I have seen women clapping their hands and tearing their clothes and crying, 'How shall we go home and see our children die in hunger? We have nothing to give them.'

It was estimated that 200,000 beggars existed in Scotland. Fletcher of Saltoun, who lived at the time, proposed selling them into slavery in the colonies as a solution. This probably happened to about 2000 individuals. Thousands immigrated to Ulster in Ireland. The population declined and Renfrewshire witnessed the last witch-hunt in the English-speaking world. Six out of the fifty accused were strangled and burned.

Scottish trade seemed to be in decline. There was a shortage of coined money because Scotland had no access to gold or silver. The Scots faced the further problem of higher tariffs (taxes) being put onto goods that they exported. Woollen cloth was banned from being exported to France after 1690. King William's wars abroad, including the Nine Years' War 1689–1697, imposed a much greater tax burden on Scotland. This was made worse by the effects of the first Jacobite Rising in 1689.

Another problem by 1700 was debt. Wealthier Scots acquired more debt because they were buying expensive luxury items. These included paintings, sculptures, chinaware, mirrors, clocks and soft furnishings amongst many other things. Possibly one quarter of all landed estates were sold between 1660 and 1710 as a result of bankruptcy.

In the Highlands, the development of a money economy from the black cattle trade created problems. In Source 1.41, the Gaelic poet Iain Lom (John MacDonald of Keppoch) criticised Angus MacDonald, Chief of Glengarry, for his new expensive lifestyle, which kept him away from his clan homeland.

Source 1.41

Iain Lom's criticism of Angus MacDonald:

'You seemed to me to be a long time in England,
being ruined by gaming [gambling].
I would prefer you in a coat and plaid [traditional Highland dress]
than in a cloak which fastens;
and that you should walk in a sprightly manner
in trews [trousers] made of tartan cloth
and visit for a spell
in grassy Glen Quoich'.

There was a growing feeling amongst Scots of 'a sinking nation' during the 1690s. This helps to explain the enthusiasm which gripped Scotland's attempt to establish its own colony at Darien. It was seen as a way of solving the nation's economic problems.

The traditional bleak picture of the Scottish economy at the start of the eighteenth century is challenged by some modern historians. They believe that the Scottish economy had weaknesses but was not crippled by the famine or the financial losses in the Darien Scheme. There was economic development and recovery by 1707. Scotland's success in international trade played an important part. To those living in the 1690s, however, it must have looked like extremely dark times indeed. There was a lack of confidence about the future. This made some Scots look towards a closer union with England as a solution to economic problems.

Activities

1 Make a wordsearch about the difficulties faced by Scotland in 1700.
   - Your wordsearch should be no more than 10 squares by 10 squares.
   - The words/phrases can go in any direction and phrases can be split.
   - Each word/phrase must have a definition or clue to help someone find the word/phrase.
   - When you have completed your puzzle, exchange it with another person and use the clues to the puzzle you receive to find the answers.

The Legislative War 1701–1705

King Carlos II of Spain died in 1700. He was deformed, with a huge head and tongue, and teeth that could not meet when his jaw closed. Carlos' inability to have children was the result of marriages between close members of the Habsburg royal family over many generations. His father and mother were uncle and niece. Carlos left the Spanish throne to Philip of Anjou, the grandson of Louis XIV of France. This event had a dramatic effect on Anglo–Scottish relations.

Source 1.42

King Carlos (Charles) of Spain ruled 1665–1700. This painting hides his deformities

In September 1701, James VII died in exile in France. Louis XIV recognised James' son (James Francis Edward Stuart) as James VIII in Scotland, James III in England and the rightful King of Britain. James VIII was known as the Old Pretender because of his claim to the throne. The English faced the possibility that the monarchies of France and Spain would be united upon Louis XIV's death. This led England into the War of the Spanish Succession 1701–1714 in order to prevent French domination of Europe.

A good overview of the War of the Spanish Succession is provided at: www.youtube.com/watch?v=4L_2tZ51C7A.

England needed Scotland to accept the English choice for the British succession. This would avoid the Scots invading England with French help, while the English fought abroad. The War of the Spanish Succession could have become the War of the British Succession if the Scots did not agree about who would be the future British monarchs.

The English Act of Settlement 1701 (see Source 1.43) decided the future of the British succession.

The English assumed that the Scots would agree to the English Act of Settlement 1701, but did not bother to ask them. This act settled the succession upon the Protestant House of Hanover from Germany. The Scots were also ignored over whether they wanted to fight in the War of the Spanish Succession. Under an act of law, the Scottish Parliament should have been summoned by the new monarch, Queen Anne, within 20 days of the death of William of Orange (on 9 March 1702) but did not meet until June 1702 – 90 days after William's death. By this time, the English Parliament had already entered the War of the Spanish Succession. Scottish sovereignty (the right to make independent decisions) had been ignored. The consequence of all this was a war of legislation between Scotland and England.

Source 1.43

English Act of Settlement 1701:

'Princess Sophia, Electress and Duchess Dowager of Hanover, daughter of… Princess Elizabeth, late Queen of Bohemia, daughter of… King James the First… is hereby declared to be the next in succession, in the Protestant line, to the imperial Crown and dignity of the said Realms of England, France, and Ireland, with the dominions and territories thereunto belonging…'

Source 1.44

The Scottish Act of Security 1703:

'Upon the death of her Majesty [Queen Anne], without heirs of her body the said successor, and the heirs of the successor's body, must be of the royal line of Scotland and of the true Protestant religion. The heir may not also be the successor to the Crown of England, unless, during her majesty's reign, acts are passed to secure the sovereignty of this crown and kingdom, the freedom, frequency and power of Parliaments, the religion, liberty and trade of the nation from English, or any foreign, influence.'

The Scottish response to the 1701 English Act of Settlement was the Scottish Act of Security 13 August 1703 (see Source 1.44).

The Act of Security was approved by the Scottish Parliament in 1703 but Queen Anne only agreed to it in 1704. The Scots wanted free trade with England and her American colonies and an end to English interference in Scottish affairs, before they would agree to the succession.

The Scots were not necessarily going to accept the same monarch as the English, unless their various grievances against the English were addressed. The Scottish Parliament refused to give England a grant of money. This would have been used to help the war against France being fought in Europe. The Scots had never before refused.

Although England was at war with France, the Scottish Wine Act 1703 allowed foreign wines, including French, to be imported into Scotland. The Wine Act was proposed by Scottish supporters of the English government. This was an attempt to try to get the Scottish Parliament to approve money for the foreign war effort.

The Act Anent Peace and War 1703 proved another annoyance to the English.

The Scottish Parliament said in their Act Anent Peace and War 1703 that it might not help England fight her foreign wars in the future. England had entered the War of the Spanish Succession in 1701, but not asked the Scottish Parliament for its agreement. The Scottish Parliament now said that it could decide its own foreign policy. This was a big problem for Queen Anne.

James Douglas (1662–1711), 2nd Duke of Queensberry, lost his position as Queen Anne's top government minister in Scotland because of what happened in the Scottish Parliament in 1703.

Source 1.45

Act Anent Peace and War 1703:

'[Queen Anne], with advice and consent of the [Scottish] Estates of Parliament… declares, that after her Majesty's death, and failing heirs of her body, no person being King or Queen of Scotland and England, shall have the sole power of making war with any prince, ruler or state whatsoever without consent of [the Scottish] Parliament; and that no declaration of war without consent, shall be binding on the subjects of this [Scottish] Kingdom.'

Queensberry was not a popular figure. Queen Anne called him 'odious': this is a word meaning offensive and repulsive. The Queen was annoyed with Queensberry for failing to control the 1703 Scottish Parliament and especially for allowing it to approve the Act of Security. This act tried to limit the monarch's power to interfere in Scottish affairs. Queen Anne wrote a letter (see Source 1.47) to Queensberry, which expressed her anger. Queensberry was sacked by Queen Anne.

Source 1.46

James Douglas, 2nd Duke of Queensberry

James Douglas, 2nd Duke of Queensberry by Godfrey Kneller, 1701–1705 © Crown copyright: UK Government Art Collection

Source 1.47

Queen Anne's letter to Queensberry:

'It seems the [Scottish] parliament has conceived a prejudice against you, and that the people slight my authority under your administration: but I will take care for the future, that neither you shall be exposed to their hatred, nor my authority to contempt.'

In 1703, Queensberry had also attempted to ruin the reputation of his opponents in the Scottish Parliament. Queensberry claimed that his opponents were involved in a Jacobite plot. This became known as 'the Scotch Plot' or 'the Queensberry Plot 1703'. The plot was clearly untrue, especially as the unpleasant Simon Fraser of Lovat had given Queensberry all the false information. Queensberry's plan did not work. The events of 1703 demonstrated to Queen Anne that the Scottish Parliament was difficult to control because different groups wanted power and influence.

On the day that the Union was passed in 1707, Queensberry's eldest son was found in the kitchen of their Edinburgh house. He was roasting a small boy, who worked in the kitchen, over an open fire. The boy was tied and being turned on a roasting pole called a spit. Queensberry's son was mentally ill. Opponents of the Union said that this was God's punishment for the Duke of Queensberry supporting the Union.

Source 1.48

Queensberry House is the big house in this background of this drawing. It is in the Canongate area of Edinburgh, near to the Scottish Parliament building. It was owned by the Duke of Queensberry. The second image shows Queensberry House as it looks today, beside the new Scottish Parliament building.

Queen Anne appointed John Hay, Earl of Tweeddale, to replace Queensberry. Tweeddale was one of the people that Queensberry had claimed was involved in the alleged Jacobite plot. Tweeddale could not prevent the 1704 Scottish Parliament passing the Wool Act.

Queen Anne only agreed to sign the Act of Security in August 1704 because she still needed the Scottish Parliament to grant money to help England's war effort in Europe. She agreed to the Scottish Wool Act of 1704, which was not in the interests of English trade, for the same reason.

By the end of the 1704 Parliament, the question of the succession had still not been agreed by the Scots. Scotland seemed to be behaving like an unreliable rogue nation. Matters were made worse by the Captain

Source 1.49

The modern historian T. Devine believes that:

'The Wool Act was regarded as openly hostile by England in allowing the export and prohibiting [banning] the import of wool. As such it was viewed as an openly aggressive act against English trade.'

Green Affair. His ship, the Worcester, was seized at Leith, outside Edinburgh. This was revenge for the English East Indies Company seizing a ship belonging to the Company of Scotland. Captain Green and two of his Worcester crew were charged with piracy. This was nonsense, but the sailors were hanged on Leith Sands on 11 April 1705, in front of a huge crowd of 80,000 people wanting revenge.

Queen Anne was only able to act against the Scots because a major victory had been won against the French at the Battle of Blenheim in August 1704. The British

Source 1.50

This ship is similar to the one that was seized from Captain Green by the Scots

Source 1.51

A ballad (song) that was written at the time of Captain Green and his crew's execution. It celebrated the event and warned other Englishmen not to do wrong to Scotland

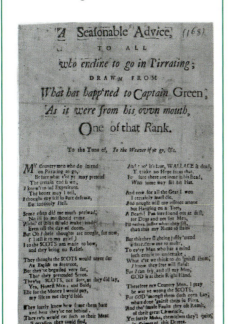

commander John Churchill, first Duke of Marlborough, was rewarded by being given Blenheim Palace, built near Oxford between 1705 and 1722.

The English Parliament passed the Alien Act in February 1705. The Act threatened to treat all Scots as foreigners in England. The key Scottish trade with England in cattle, linen, coal and sheep was banned unless negotiations for a full union started by 25 December 1706. This would settle the succession and end the difficulties of managing Scottish affairs because the Scottish Parliament would no longer exist. This would also avoid any of Queen Anne's successors having to agree to limitations being imposed upon their royal powers.

Source 1.52

Blenheim Palace near Oxford, England. It is a smaller version of the royal family's Buckingham Palace. How can you tell that the Duke of Marlborough's victory at Blenheim was important?

Source 1.53

The Alien Act 1705:

'That from and after the 25 day of December 1705, no person or persons being a native or natives of the Kingdom of Scotland shall be capable to inherit any lands within this Kingdom of England or to enjoy any benefit or advantage of a natural-born subject of England: But every such person shall be from henceforth adjudged and taken as an alien, until such time as the Succession to the Crown of Scotland, be declared and settled by an Act of Parliament in Scotland [and] no great cattle or sheep shall be brought out of or from the Kingdom of Scotland into the Kingdom of England or Ireland, Dominion of Wales or town of Berwick upon Tweed; no Scotch coals shall be imported out of the Kingdom of Scotland no Scotch linen shall be imported or brought out of Scotland.'

Activity

1. This activity will help make the opening sections about the problems in Anglo–Scottish relations more memorable. For this activity you need to make a spider diagram around the main theme of problems in Anglo–Scottish relations. The diagram has been started for you below, but you need to develop the other boxes by drawing extra legs and entering relevant information. Use the whole of Chapter 1 to help you.

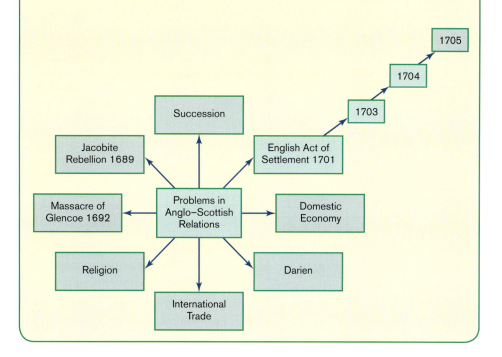

2 Arguments For and Against the Union

England's Arguments for Union

On four occasions between 1660 and 1702, the Scots attempted a closer union with England, but failed. This would suggest that the attitude of England was important in securing a full incorporating union in 1707.

Scotland was viewed as a poor northern neighbour and a closer association between the two countries offered England no advantage. Sir Edward Seymour, the Tory Leader in the English House of Commons, said of Scotland in 1700 that 'whoever married a beggar could only expect a louse for her portion' (Quoted in Devine, 2004), meaning a louse to suck your blood.

Queen Anne (see Source 2.1) reigned from 8 March 1702 until 1 August 1714. She visited her Scottish kingdom only once in 1681 as a 16 year old. At her coronation, Anne had medals distributed to the guests with 'Entirely English' written on them.

England increasingly feared being invaded by Scotland while fighting the French abroad. England fought France a total of six times between 1702 and 1815. The War of the Spanish Succession was the first war against the French. It lasted from 1701–1714.

Source 2.1

'these strange [Scottish] people', 'these unreasonable Scotsmen', 'I know my heart to be entirely English' – these quotations are from Queen Anne. She never bothered to be crowned in Scotland

Source 2.2

Jonathan Swift, an English government supporter, points out the military threat posed to England by the Scots choosing their own king:

'It was thought highly dangerous to leave that part of the Island inhabited by a poor, fierce Northern People, at liberty to put themselves under a different King and so the union became necessary, not for any actual good it could possibly do us [England], but to avoid a probable evil.'

Source 2.3

Daniel Defoe wrote:

'It could not be expected that England, whose considerations for uniting were peace, strength and shutting a back door of continual war and confusion from the north, should communicate [grant] trade, freedom of customs [taxes] in all her ports and plantations [colonies], with import and export of manufactures [goods], and leave the main things yet precarious and uncertain.'

Daniel Defoe was an English spy in Scotland. In Source 2.3 he makes it clear that only a full Union offered England military security. Only then would England allow the Scots to have access to the English colonies and free trade.

The English started to support a Union with Scotland after 1700 for another good reason. Their international trade was threatened by the success of the Scots, especially in America. England's population was not growing and this was a problem if England wanted to continue the expansion and protection of her empire against competitors.

Source 2.4 was written by a modern historian. In a full Union Scottish manpower would be a useful contribution to England's wars, colonies and manufacturing. Scotland was an obvious choice to solve these English problems because she was Protestant.

Source 2.4

Professor A.I. Macinnes argues:

'The key was not just political security during the War of the Spanish Succession but also colonial security, particularly in the Americas, where Scottish commercial [trading] networks, no less than plantations [settlements], had proved a more disruptive and predatory [plundering] influence than the Irish. Union sought to channel such entrepreneurship [activity] into imperial service. The English priority in seeking Union was to secure Scottish labour for English wars, colonies and manufacture, not necessarily to promote manufacturing to retain labour within Scotland.'

After 1707, England's foreign wars became British ones, with Scottish soldiers playing a key role. The British Army Colonel in Canada, James Wolfe, wrote a letter dated 9 June 1751 in which he referred to the Scottish Highlander troops under his command as first class soldiers because they were 'hardy, intrepid [brave], accustomed to rough country and no great mischief if they fall' (Quoted in Hunter, 1995).

Scottish soldiers were important to the English and then British Empire. The modern historian Professor N. Ferguson has researched Scottish casualties in World War I (1914–1918). He believes that 'The Scots were (after the Serbs and the Turks) the soldiers who suffered the highest death rate of the war' (Ferguson, 1999). Scottish soldiers were so well thought of that they were often sent first into battle – this explains the high death rates. As you learned in the previous section, the threat posed by the Scottish Parliament to royal authority concerned Queen Anne and the English Government. They did not want limitations being imposed upon the power of future monarchs by a Scottish Parliament.

From an English viewpoint, the Union of 1707 served their military, trading and political interests first and foremost.

Activities

1. You are working for the English Government in 1705. You have been asked to prepare a report recommending whether or not the Government should support a full incorporating union. In your report you should:

   - recommend whether or not a full union should be introduced
   - provide arguments to support your conclusions
   - identify and comment on any arguments which may be presented by those who oppose your recommendation.

   In your report you must use extensive background knowledge. You should use information from pages 20–23 and 32–42 to help you. Your report should include information on:

   - dealing with the military threat from Scotland
   - the international trade threat from Scotland
   - England's population problem and the threat to royal authority posed by the Scottish Parliament.

2. You may be requested to present your report in written form or as a spoken presentation lasting between two and four minutes.

Scottish Arguments against Union

How did most Scots feel about the Treaty of Union?

The Union came into effect on 1 May 1707. The bells of St. Giles Church in Edinburgh played the tune 'How can I be sad upon my Wedding Day?'

There is considerable evidence of popular opposition to the Union. This was sometimes based on an anti-English feeling called Anglophobia.

During the debate about the Treaty of Union in the Scottish Parliament, petitions against the Union arrived from all over Scotland. The Duke of Argyll, who supported Union, suggested that they should be made into kites!

Source 2.5

The view of one Scottish pamphlet about English people during the Union debate:

'a pack of pock pudding, pork eaters, belly-god tykes [dogs]… the refuse of the whole earth, a hotch potch of bastardly, dastardly scum, sprung from the armies that subdued England from time to time.'

Source 2.6 shows which parts of Scotland sent petitions against Union. The Court Party were unable to get any petitions of their own showing support for Union.

Source 2.6

The parts of Scotland that petitioned against Union

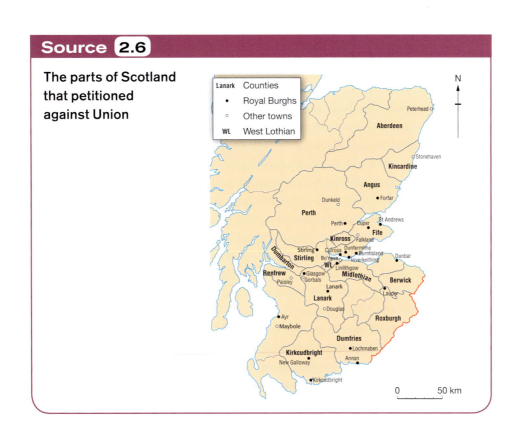

Arguments For and Against the Union

Some modern historians suggest that support for Union may have been underestimated and opposition overstated, but there is agreement that the majority of popular opinion remained against the Union. There were riots in Dumfries, Stirling and Glasgow. Copies of the terms of Union were burned.

On 23 October 1706, the house of the Lord Provost, a Scottish Commissioner and Union supporter, was stormed by the Edinburgh mob.

Source 2.7 was written by the English spy Daniel Defoe. He wrote that there was a 'General Aversion' to Union in Scotland. His letter captures a sense of the atmosphere in Edinburgh at this time.

Source 2.7

Daniel Defoe wrote:
'I found the whole city in a most dreadful uproar and the high street full of the rabble. I heard a great noise and looking out saw a terrible multitude come up the high street with a drum at the head of them shouting and swearing and crying out all Scotland would stand together, No Union, No Union, English Dogs, and the like.'

What were the Scots worried about in a full, incorporating Union?

The 91 petitions received by the Scottish Parliament expressed a number of concerns about a full Union. They included increased taxation, competition from English trade, the loss of sovereignty (independence) and national identity, along with laws and liberties and fears about religion.

Source 2.8 is a petition against a full, incorporating Union from the General Convention of the Royal Burghs dated 29 October 1706. It feared that Scottish trade would be disadvantaged by English taxes and laws because English MPs would be in the majority in the new British Parliament.

Source 2.8

Petition from the General Convention of the Royal Burghs, 29 October 1706:
'Our Monarchy is suppressed, our Parliament extinguished, and in consequence our religion, church government, Claim of Right, laws, liberties, trade, and all that is dear to us, daily in danger of being altered by the English, in a British Parliament. And by these articles our poor people are made liable to the English taxes, which is a certain unsupportable burden. And considering that the most considerable branches of our trade are differing from those of England, and are yet more discouraged as the Parliament of Great Britain shall think fit.'

What were the attractions of a Federal Union for the Scots?

Scottish concerns about a full Union led to the idea of a federal Union as an alternative. A federal Union was one in which Scotland would keep its own Parliament, laws and church. There would, however, be co-operation and agreement between Scotland and England about trade and other issues. The idea of a federal union was written about by James Hodges.

> ### Source 2.9
>
> In *The Rights and Interests of the Two British Monarchies* Hodges argues that only a federal union would allow Scottish interests to be protected:
>
> 'There is a proposal for a federal union under one monarch. In it, there shall be no other alteration in the constitutions of either kingdom, but that each are to retain their national distinctions, to enjoy their particular liberties, privileges, and independence, and to hold their different governments in Church and State, with the laws, customs and rights of the same, as they did before the Union. This kind of union is different from that, which some insist upon for uniting the two into one kingdom, one government, one parliament etc. under the title of an incorporating union.
>
> A federal union is much more agreeable to the real interests of both nations. But it is simply impossible to consult the true interests of either nation by an incorporating union.'

What did Andrew Fletcher of Saltoun (1653–1716) argue?

Andrew Fletcher wanted the Scottish Parliament to have greater powers and the monarchy and nobility to have less, but he was not a republican. Fletcher wanted a constitutional monarchy. This is a monarchy with a written constitution. Fletcher viewed the English Alien Act 1705 (see page 38) as an abuse of royal power. This helps to explain his 1705 proposal of 12 limitations on royal and noble powers. A desire to limit royal power also lay behind Fletcher's support for the Act of Security 1703 and Act Anent Peace and War 1703.

Source 2.10

Fletcher of Saltoun (1653–1716) opposed the Union

Fletcher argued that Scotland should keep its independence because its interests would not be considered in an English-dominated British Parliament.

Some historians believe that Fletcher anticipated the kind of arrangement that exists today in the European Union. In Fletcher's view, countries, including Scotland, would keep their independence but co-operate internationally to promote trade and peace. His ideas are known to have inspired the American President Thomas Jefferson. Fletcher is regarded by some Scots as a hero because he opposed the Union and defended Scottish independence.

Source 2.11

Extract from Fletcher's *The State of the Controversy Betwixt United and Separate Parliaments* (1706):

'In the most absolute and incorporate union that can be made betwixt [between] these two nations, there are several interests which are and must be reserved separate to each nation. It seems beyond human comprehension, how these separate distinct interests can be regulated and supported by one Parliament. For the Scots to subject these interests to a united Parliament is so far from being a way to avoid English influence that it is the way to throw themselves headlong into it. The Scots deserve no pity, if they voluntarily surrender their united and separate interests to the mercy of a united Parliament, where the English shall have so vast a majority.'

In Source 2.12 Fletcher used Wales as an example to show that a full Union with England did not guarantee improved trade and economic prosperity.

Source 2.12

Fletcher argued:

'Wales, the only country that ever united with England, lying at less distance from London, and… [more able]… to participate in the circulation of a great trade than we do, after three or four hundred years, is still the only place of that kingdom, which has no considerable commerce, though possessed of one of the best ports in the whole island; a sufficient demonstration that trade is not a necessary consequence of an union with England.'

Fletcher's own manner and personality caused him problems and eventually led to a loss of influence. He had a hot temper and offered to fight duels to resolve differences. He threatened to tie the Earl of Stair to a horse's tail and have him dragged through the streets of Edinburgh. Fletcher also made bad political decisions, such as supporting the disastrous Protestant Monmouth Rebellion against James VII in 1685. It was also said that Fletcher had shot dead a local man after an argument about a horse during this rebellion.

What role did religion have in opposing the Union?

The section on religion on pages 14–19 in Chapter 1 explained the differences between Presbyterians, Episcopalians and Catholics. Religion influenced Scottish attitudes towards Union with England. The flow chart below summarises the different religious views of Union.

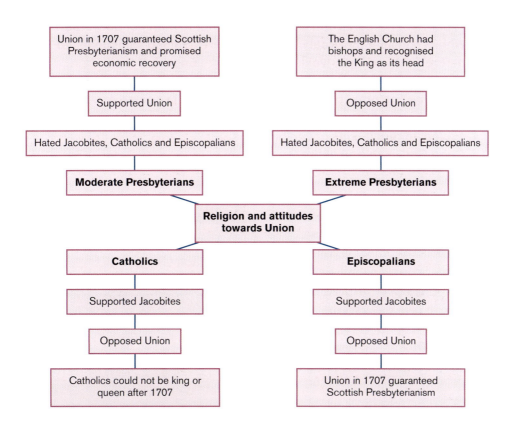

What role did self-interest have in opposing the Union?

Personal selfishness also played a part in arguments against the Union. The 2nd Lord Belhaven (John Hamilton) argued that a full Union would bring complete disaster for Scotland (See Source 2.13).

Belhaven ended his speech on both his knees and in tears but inside the Scottish Parliament it had little impact. When Belhaven had finished speaking the Earl of Marchmont, who supported Union, said about Belhaven, 'Behold he dreamed, but lo! When he awoke, he found it was a dream' (Quoted in Magnusson, 2001).

Parliament ended that session in laughter.

Source 2.13

Belhaven's speech to the Scottish Parliament in 1706:

'I think I see the royal state of burghs walking their desolate streets, hanging down their heads under disappointments. I think I see the honest, industrious tradesman, loaded with new taxes and impositions, drinking water in place of ale, eating his saltless pottage [a vegetable based, meatless soup], petitioning for encouragement to his manufactories [making goods by hand]...
I think I see the laborious ploughman, with his corn spoiling upon his hands for want of sale, cursing the day of his birth, dreading the expense of his burial and uncertain whether to marry or do worse. When I consider this treaty, as it has been explained and spoken to before us these three weeks past, I see the English Constitution remaining firm, the same two Houses of Parliament, the same taxes, the same customs [taxes on imported goods], the same excises [taxes on goods made in Scotland and then sold], and all ours either subject to regulations or annihilations.
Good God. Is this an entire surrender?'

Some modern historians believe that Belhaven's career was limited because of his own selfishness. When Belhaven showed concern for ordinary Scottish people in a full Union others were surprised. He had refused to help the starving poor in his parish of Spott during the famine in the 1690s and had also voted in favour of Article 15 of Union, the Equivalent, which offered compensation for those who had invested in the Darien Scheme. He was an investor!

Source 2.14

James Hamilton, 4th Duke of Hamilton (1658–1712)

Another man thought to be operating for selfish motives was James Hamilton, 4th Duke of Hamilton (1658–1712), shown in Source 2.14. Hamilton was leader of the opposition against Union in the Scottish Parliament, yet he let down his own side more than once. Opponents of Union were shocked when Hamilton allowed Queen Anne to appoint the Scottish Commissioners to discuss the Union terms. Later, during a crucial discussion about the terms of the Union, Hamilton failed to turn up because he claimed to have toothache – and after the Union was passed

Hamilton was rewarded by the Queen with the title the Duke of Brandon. Hamilton had debts to pay off and there is evidence to suggest that he was co-operating with the government during the Union debate.

Why did the opposition to Union fail?

Opposition to Union was never strongly united. Different groups had different reasons for being against the Union. In December 1706 a planned rising of 7000–8000 Highland Jacobites and Covenanters from the south-west of Scotland did not take place. There was just too much of a difference in beliefs between the two groups.

The Duke of Hamilton's leadership as the head of the opposition to Union was also ineffective. Some opponents of Union merely went home after Article 8 was voted upon. Other opponents turned up late or not at all.

As you will find out in Chapter 3, the Articles of Union also seemed to address Scottish concerns about a full Union. A number of amendments to the Treaty terms were made. Some historians see this as a genuine response to popular opinion. Alterations to the Treaty terms also reinforced the belief that Union was a good deal.

Popular opposition to Union as a whole was, however, ignored. The issues of national identity and loss of sovereignty (parliament and independence) were not enough on their own to defeat the Union being passed in the Scottish Parliament. The decisive factor in passing the Union was perhaps the supporters of the Union being a far more united body throughout the Union debate.

Activities

1. Prepare to make a speech (lasting no less than one minute and no more than two) outlining why a full Union should be opposed in 1707. What points would you make in order to have the broadest possible appeal to all the groups who might oppose Union in 1707? No racism is allowed. Your success criteria is to include the following:

   - fears about trade
   - loss of sovereignty and identity
   - loss of liberties and laws
   - English interests being put first in a British Parliament
   - a dislike of England by Scottish working people in the 1700s
   - a desire to have greater powers for the Scottish Parliament and reduce the power of the monarch and nobility
   - fears about religion for moderate and extreme Presbyterians and Episcopalians

   continued

Activities continued

- the advantages of a federal Union
- the Jacobite desire to restore the House of Stuart.

2 Prepare a spider diagram around the central heading 'Why the opponents of Union failed'. You must have at least five labelled legs. Each reason should be boxed and coloured differently from the rest.

Scottish Arguments for Union

There are many reasons explaining why a majority of Scottish politicians supported a full incorporating Union with England in 1707.

Economic reasons

Some Scots believed that Scotland's economy would improve if they supported a full Union with England. Fifteen of the final 25 Articles of Union passed in 1707 were about economic issues. Article 4 of the Treaty of Union granted free trade within the UK and all British colonies abroad, including America. This was the Article which received the biggest support from the Scottish Parliament, with a 156 to 19 vote in its favour.

Source 2.15

John Clerk of Penicuik (1676–1755)

John Clerk of Penicuik (1676–1755) was one of the Scottish Commissioners who negotiated the terms of Union. They were taken back to the Scottish Parliament for debate. Clerk supported a full incorporating Union and published a book about it. Probably to avoid criticism, he did not want the book published during his

Source 2.16

John Clerk wrote:

'Some are regretting the extreme poverty of the nation, and scarcity of money. It is scarce conceivable how any condition of life we can fall into, can render us more miserable and poor than we are. For it's very well known that many of us live with difficulty, and many thousands of our nearest relations are obliged to leave [emigrate] their country for want of bread and employment.'

lifetime, wrote it in Latin and hid it down a coal mine as the Jacobites approached Edinburgh in 1745.

John Clerk saw a full Union as the only way for the Scottish economy to recover from the bad experience of the 1690s. He believed that there was no other option available, except a full Union with England.

Daniel Defoe tried to convince the Scots that only in a full Union could Scotland expect equal treatment with England in terms of trade. Defoe pointed out that when James VI of Scotland became the first British monarch (when he was crowned James I of England in 1603) English influence on the monarch became greater because the Scottish royal court moved to London. Defoe argued that this disadvantage would end with a full and equal Union.

Source 2.17

Daniel Defoe wrote:
'The Scots had been very conscious of the visible decay of trade, wealth and inhabitants in their country… The sinking condition of their nation was plainly due to the loss of their court [with the Union of Crowns 1603], the disadvantages of trade and the influence the English had over their kings.'

Source 2.18 is from a speech by Seton of Pitmedden (c.1639–1719). He was a Scottish Commissioner in the Union negotiations and supported a full incorporating Union. He argued in favour of gaining access to England's empire because Scotland could not do this as an independent country. Union also guaranteed security against Catholic France.

Source 2.18

Seton of Pitmedden's speech:
'If we attempt the East-Indies trade, that is already enhanced [controlled] by the Dutch, English, French, Spaniards, or Portuguese, from whom we must expect opposition, they themselves opposing one another daily.
The trade of Africa is, for the most part, of small value; and every province of America is claimed as property, by some powerful European nation.
From these considerations, I conceive that this nation [Scotland], by an entire separation from England, cannot extend its trade, so as to raise its power in proportion to other trafficking [trading] nations in Europe.'

Source 2.19 is a modern photograph of Seton of Pitmedden's country estate. He had a keen interest in agricultural improvement. Like many of the wealthy landowners who supported the Union, he had little or no understanding of the highly successful illegal overseas trade between Scotland and the American colonies. This led landowners like Pitmedden to see a full Union with England as the only option available.

Source 2.19

Seton of Pitmedden's country estate

When Seton of Pitmedden made the speech in Source 2.20, he was probably referring to the opposition of William and the English to the Scottish Darien Scheme, along with the English Navigation Acts. These acts had banned Scottish trade with the American colonies.

Source 2.20

Pitmedden argued that the English would only grant the Scots access to their colonies in a full incorporating Union:

'Every monarch, having two or more kingdoms, will be obliged to prefer the counsel and interest of the stronger to that of the weaker: and the greater disparity [difference] of power and riches there is betwixt [between] these Kingdoms, the greater influence the more powerful nation will have on the sovereign [monarch]. This nation being poor and without force to protect it, its commerce [trade] cannot reap great advantages by it, till it partake of the trade and protection of some powerful neighbour nation, that can communicate [give] both these.'

Source 2.21

A petition from the Burgh of Montrose in favour of the Union, 15 October 1706:

'Unless there is a Union, the English will undoubtedly bring back the laws which were repealed last session... And then one needs not the gift of prophecy to foretell what shall be the fate of this poor miserable nation in a few years.'

The Burgh of Montrose supported Union because they did not want the Alien Act of 1705 to be put into practice. This would have banned Scottish exports to England if a full Union was not agreed.

The Succession and Protestantism

A Protestant monarch was guaranteed in the Treaty of Union. This would secure the Presbyterian religion in Scotland. England's protection against the threat of Catholic France was also guaranteed. James Ogilvie, 1st Earl of Seafield, makes these points in Source 2.22. He was Chancellor in Scotland from 1702–4 and 1705–8. He supported a full incorporating Union, but some modern historians believe that he was corrupt and self-seeking.

Source 2.22

James Ogilvie, 1st Earl of Seafield, argued:

'My reasons for conjoining with England on good terms were these: that the kingdom of England is a Protestant kingdom and that the joining with them was a security for our religion. England has trade and other advantages to give us, which no other kingdom could afford. England has freedom and liberty, and that the joining with it was the best way to secure that to us and that I saw no other method for securing our peace, the two kingdoms being in the same island, and foreign assistance was both dangerous to ourselves and England and that I was for the treaty.'

An Act for Securing the Protestant Religion and Presbyterian Church Government was passed on 12 November 1706. This ended fears about the Church of Scotland's status after Union and meant that its opposition to Union ended. This was a key moment. Moderate Presbyterians were reassured and gave their support to passing the Union.

Source 2.23

The English spy, Daniel Defoe, makes clear his awareness of the importance that religion played in the Union being passed:

'The most dangerous rock of difference, on which the Union could split, and which could now render it ineffectual, was that of religion.'

Military invasion and civil war

The Scots were aware of the increased military power of England. This was shown by the Duke of Marlborough's impressive victories over the French at Blenheim in 1704 and Ramillies in 1706. Ireland had already been conquered by the English and made into a province. This meant that the Irish had been excluded from England's colonial trade with America. The Scots knew this. The Scots feared an English military invasion if they rejected the Union. The Scots wanted to avoid being treated like Ireland.

Source 2.24

The Earl of Roxburgh wrote this on 15 December 1705:

'If Union fail, war will never be avoided; and for my part the more I think of Union, the more I like it, seeing no security anywhere else.'

John Clerk of Penicuik supported the Union because he was keen to avoid a civil war in Scotland, Ireland and England, as had happened in the 1640s. He also did not want a military conquest of Scotland if Union was rejected by the Scots. Conquest had already happened in the 1650s under the brutal English General Oliver Cromwell.

Source 2.25

John Clerk wrote:

'Many in Scotland expected such a scene of misfortunes as had been felt during the Civil Wars in the reign of King Charles the First and in the end that the whole country would fall under the dominion of England by right of conquest. The Union of the two kingdoms was then thought of as the best expedient [method] to preserve the honour and liberties of Scotland and likewise the peace of the whole island, for as the councils of Britain would then be united, the succession would naturally devolve on one and the same person. This was the principal motive both in Scotland and England for bringing about the Union.'

During the debate about the Union in the Scottish Parliament, a large English army was on the border of Scotland and England. There was also another one in Ireland. Modern historians disagree about the importance of the presence of these armies.

> **Source 2.26**
>
> Professor C. Whatley states:
>
> 'There is no documentary evidence to suggest that it was the prospect of being run through with English steel that persuaded [Scottish] parliamentarians to approve union.'

> **Source 2.27**
>
> Professor A.I. Macinnes notes:
>
> 'All parties in Scotland, however, were conscious that England had the military and fiscal [financial] resources to rerun the Cromwellian Union of the 1650s.'

The best terms possible

The Treaty of Union gave the Scots compensation for Darien and access to England's colonies. The Scots had tried but failed to get these terms in the negotiations for Union in 1702. The 1707 Union seemed to be a success.

There were also amendments made to the Articles of Union as they were debated. Presbyterianism and the Church of Scotland were guaranteed as well. Those who voted for the Union thought that they were getting the best deal possible.

Principles

The Scottish MPs who supported the Union had beliefs. These are called principles. A computer analysis of how politicians voted in the Scottish Parliament on each article of the Treaty of Union shows that 'principle' was important to both the supporters and opponents of the Union. Voting for your principles means that you do what you genuinely believe to be right. Each issue in the Union debate seems to have been considered upon its own worth.

The Court Party in Scotland supported the Union. Their name was taken from their support of the monarch's government ministers at court. The Court Party had supported the revolution of 1689 and wanted to keep the power of the monarch. They were Presbyterian and saw the chance to get good job positions within the Empire. The Scottish Court Party co-operated with the political group in England known as the Whigs. Together they achieved a full incorporating Union. This meant the end of the Scottish Parliament's existence.

The Squadrone Volante was a group of about 30 Scottish MPs who supported the acts passed by the Scottish Parliament in 1703 (see Chapter 1). During the Union debate in 1706–7 they supported a full union. Their Latin name 'the Flying Squadron' was given because they changed sides. They supported the Hanoverians because this prevented the return of the Catholic Stuarts. The Squadrone members were moderate Presbyterians who opposed

an Episcopalian church and the Jacobites. Their view of Scotland's future was one based upon agriculture and manufacturing rather than overseas trade. They thought that the terms of Union were a good deal for Scotland.

Patrick Hume was a member of the Squadrone Volante. Like others in this group, he had suffered under James VII for his religious beliefs. Hume was a moderate Presbyterian. He was imprisoned for five years for his beliefs but escaped to the Netherlands in 1686. He became an advisor to William of Orange and later Lord Chancellor of Scotland (1696) under King William and Queen Mary. He was given the title the Earl of Marchmont in 1697.

Personal vested self-interest

Scottish politicians in 1707 also had a desire to benefit personally. This is called personal vested self-interest.

> **Source 2.29**
>
> Professor C. Whatley writes:
>
> 'Most Scottish politicians were calculating and opportunistic, many were two-faced and treacherous; nor were they always particularly pleasant. A very few were mad, or at least thought to be.'

Source 2.28

Patrick Hume, Earl of Marchmont

Some of those who voted for Union probably did so to benefit themselves. George MacKenzie, the 1st Earl of Cromartie, wanted to do away with the names Scotland and England and only use Britain instead. He may have been trying to advance his own career by showing support for the Union.

Some of the Scottish politicians who voted for the Union were far from angels in their personal lives. John Ker, the 5th Earl of Roxburghe, was treated for sexually transmitted diseases, which included gonorrhoea, on three separate occasions. He took mercury in an attempt to cure syphilis. He then tried praying and a better quality condom made out of rabbit skin.

The 5th Earl of Roxburghe (c.1680–1741) was a leading member of the group called the Squadrone Volante in the Scottish Parliament. Their support for the Union was crucial to it being approved. He was granted a dukedom by Queen Anne for his support of the Union. As the 1st Duke of Roxburghe he had Floors Castle built (1718–1740) to celebrate.

Source 2.30

Floors Castle

Those who supported Union thought that they were making the best decision for Scotland, but they also expected to benefit personally.

The two tables below show how each of the three Scottish estates voted on Article I of Union and the final approval of the treaty.

Article I of Union	For	Against
Nobility	46	21
Barons (gentry)	37	33
Burgesses (burghs)	33	29
Total	116	83

The final vote passing the terms of Union	For	Against
Nobility	42	19
Barons (gentry)	38	30
Burgesses (burghs)	30	20
Total	110	69

The big Scottish landowners (nobility) supported each of the terms of Union by a majority of 2:1. The nobility were the most anglicised section of

Scottish society and perhaps had the least fear about a full incorporating Union with England. The terms of Union also guaranteed the traditional powers of the landed class. Leading Scottish nobles had intermarried with English families. The Campbells even added an anglicised 'p' to their name and referred to themselves as North British!

The gentry voting may have been partly influenced by the particular trade in which individuals were involved and whether they thought Union would bring benefits. Inland burghs were less likely to support Union than those on the coast. This may reflect what the burghs thought about the possible benefits from overseas trade.

The benefits of Empire

The empire offered opportunities for career advancement, especially in the army. Just before 1707 Scots made up 10 per cent of senior officers in the British army. A colonel is a senior army officer. In 1704 there were 10,000 Scots fighting in Flanders (Belgium) with the British army. Most of the 44 nobles who supported the first Article of Union either were serving or had close male relatives in the British army. Only two of 21 nobles voting against this Article were in the army.

Activities

1. You need to read and learn the bullet point summary below.

   Reasons why some Scottish politicians supported the Union:

   - To improve the Scottish economy, especially by having access to trade with the American colonies.
   - Scotland would be treated as an equal trading partner with England and not opposed as a competitor.
   - Scotland, with English help, would be able to compete with international rivals.
   - No other option seemed to be available because this was what the English wanted.
   - Some wealthy Scottish landowners did not fully understand the Scottish economy, especially the role of overseas trade. They saw the terms of Union as a good deal.
   - Union would avoid the Alien Act of 1705 being reintroduced.
   - Protestantism and a Protestant Succession were secured in a full Union.

   continued

Activities continued

- English invasion and conquest, accompanied by civil war, could happen if Union failed to be accepted.
- Union offered security from a French Catholic and/or Jacobite invasion.
- A belief existed that the best terms possible were being negotiated, especially as amendments were made.
- An element of personal selfishness existed. Jobs and careers within the British Empire, especially in the army, were possible. Landowners seemed to have the least to fear. Some gentry and burgh representatives may have looked at the personal benefits of Union.
- Before 1706–7 a genuine desire for a closer union with England existed amongst some influential Scots.
- Some Scottish politicians and English Whigs started to agree about the future. This included no more restrictions upon the monarch's power in a full and equal Union.

2 You are required to write a speech of between 3 and 4 minutes as though it was 1707. Your speech should try to convince the Scottish Parliament to vote for the Union. You need to use all of the bullet points above in your speech. You need to explain them and not just list them. Close this book after you have learned the bullet points because you are not allowed to look at them while you are writing your final speech! A memory map of your proposed structure might be a useful way of planning your speech.

3 After you have written your speech, deliver it to others in your class. Decide in advance as a class how it will be judged – remember that part of the judgement should include a score for how many of the bullet points you included.

The Passing of the Treaty of Union

Bribery: Bought and Sold for English Gold?

Was £20,000 used as bribery?

George Lockhart of Carnwath found out about the distribution of a secret sum of £20,000 at the time of the Union debate. This created the belief that large numbers of the Scottish Parliament were bribed into voting for the 1707 Union. The accuracy of this belief is questionable.

Source 3.1

George Lockhart of Carnwath wrote this. He was a Jacobite and hated the Union so his account is biased:

'Money was sent to Scotland from England and employed in bribing Members of Parliament. It was discovered and reported back to the British parliament by the commissioners appointed by parliament that a sum of 20,000 pounds sterling was sent by the Treasury of England to the Earl of Glasgow in the Year of 1706. It is abundantly disgraceful for anyone to contribute to the misery and ruin of his native country. But if persons of quality and distinction sell, and even at so cheap a price, themselves and their descendents, let their memories be hateful to all future generations.'

Source 3.2

Taken from 'Song Against the Union' written by Iain Lom (John MacDonald of Keppoch). He was a Jacobite poet and believed that greedy Lowland nobles were bribed into voting for Union:

'Lord Dupplin, without delay
the vent to your throat opened,
a turbulence rose in your heart
when you heard the gold coming;
you swallowed the hiccoughs of avarice [greed],
your lungs inflated and swelled,
control over your gullet [stomach] was relaxed,
and the traces of your arse were unloosed'.

The idea that bribery influenced the voting of Scottish Parliament members was widespread at the time. The eighteenth-century writers Robert Burns and Sir Walter Scott also believed that bribery was used in 1707, as do some modern historians, including P.H. Scott and W. Ferguson.

Some modern historians now argue that the £20,000 was genuinely paid for salaries that were still owed. This is called arrears of salary.

R. Mitchison is a modern historian. She thinks that the £20,000 was too small to be anything but genuine payment for arrears of salary (see Source 3.4). The messenger who carried the Treaty of Union was paid £60. This was more than some of those who received money from the £20,000.

The table in Source 3.5 shows members of the different political groups who received money from the £20,000.

Source 3.3

Robert Burns' (1759–96) poem 'A Parcel of Rogues' refers to the 1707 Union. The words are now well known as a folk song. You can find the complete poem on the Internet. Here is an extract:

> 'We're bought and sold for English gold –
> Such a parcel of rogues in a nation!'

Source 3.4

R. Mitchison writes:

> 'The distribution of honours and money on this occasion was small. Some peerages were given, and some payment of arrears and salary, amounting in all to £20000, were secretly made. The sums were small even in terms in which the parliamentary classes worked. Their smallness suggests that they really were arrears and not bribes.'

Source 3.5

Party Office Profile

	All	Court	Squadrone	Country
Office	111	75	7	29
Arrears	69	48	5	16
Unpaid	50	35	1	14
Paid	27	20	5	2

If the £20,000 was a bribe, then it would have made more sense to have given far more to members of the opposition Country Party because they were against Union. Only two members of the Country Party received money. One was the Earl of Atholl. He received £1,000 and still voted against the Union! The other, Lord Elibank, decided to vote for Union before he knew about any money. Four individuals who had not attended the last Scottish Parliament in 1706–7 also received money. The Earls of Montrose and Roxburghe in the Squadrone Volante received £200 and £500 respectively. They had no recorded arrears, but were owed money from having held previous government jobs. It is also believed that the longer a politician had been a Member of Parliament, the more likely they were to vote for the Union. This had nothing to do with bribery.

The modern historian Professor A. I. Macinnes thinks that Scottish politicians were incompetent rather than corrupt because of the terms of Union that they agreed to.

Source 3.6

Professor A. I. Macinnes argues:

'Intent on political incorporation [Union], the English ministry were prepared to use the resources of the English Treasury to influence Scottish politics. A sum of £20,000 was eventually advanced to selectively meet arrears of salaries and pensions for Scottish politicians, arrears that were on the whole genuine not fabricated [invented]. However, the Scottish politicians who treated for union in 1706 were not a parcel of rogues bought and sold for English gold. They were not corrupt, but they were inept [incompetent]. Their ineptitude was manifested [made clear] by their negotiating stance on colonial access, reparations [Darien] and investment in manufactures.'

The £20,000 was mostly given to those who were going to vote for Union in any case. In this sense it was a reward to loyal supporters for money that they were already owed and not a bribe.

Was the Equivalent a bribe?

Article 15 of the Treaty of Union spoke about the Equivalent. This money amounted to 398,085 pounds and 10 shillings – about £56 million pounds in money today. It was designed to provide compensation for the investors in the Darien Scheme and to help the Scots pay a share of England's national debt. The money was also meant to encourage manufacturing. Some people argue that this was a bribe to vote for the Union but this argument is questionable.

> **Source 3.7**
>
> From George Lockhart of Carnwath's *Scotland's Ruine* (1714):
>
> 'But the Equivalent was the mighty bait, for here with the sum of three hundred and ninety one thousand and eighty five pounds sterling to be sent in cash to Scotland. However, the Scots were to pay it and much more back again in a few years by agreeing to bear a share of the burdens imposed on England and used for payment of England's debts. This may chiefly explain why so many of them agreed to this union. The hopes of recovering what they had spent on the Company of Scotland [Darien], and of paying debts and arrears due to them made many overlook the general interest of their country.'

It must be remembered that Lockhart, as a Jacobite, provides a one-sided account about the use of the Equivalent as bribery.

The modern historian W. Ferguson also believes that the Equivalent was used as a bribe. He maintains that the group in the Scottish Parliament known as the Squadrone Volante voted for Union because they would control who got money from the Equivalent. The Squadrone's support of the Union was vital. If they had voted against Article I of the Union it would have failed to pass and the Union would not have happened.

> **Source 3.8**
>
> W. Ferguson writes:
>
> 'The Equivalent, indeed, had a major part to play in predisposing [getting members] to favour the treaty. The Squadrone [Volante] was gulled [tricked] into the Court's interest by a promise, later broken, that as nominees of the directors of the Company of Scotland, they would be allowed to handle that part of the Equivalent intended to recoup [compensate] the shareholders.'

However, the leader of the Squadrone, the Earl of Roxburghe, had no involvement in the Darien Scheme. It seems more likely that the Squadrone decided to support Union because they had achieved the Union terms that they wanted. Their moderate Presbyterian beliefs meant that they feared the Jacobites more than Union.

A number of Squadrone members also had ties with support for William in the 1689 Revolution. They were unlikely to vote against Union. In fact, those MPs who had not invested in the Darien Scheme were more likely to vote for the Union than against which means the Equivalent was not a bribe because it did not change voting behaviour.

Were pensions, promotions and job positions used as bribes?

There is no doubt that pensions, promotions and job positions were given out at the time of the Union debate. Andrew Fletcher of Saltoun believed that it was not in the interest of anyone to oppose the Union if they cared for their future career because pensions, promotions and government jobs were controlled by the English court. Fletcher saw this as a bribe.

Source 3.9

Andrew Fletcher of Saltoun stated:

'Let no man say that it cannot be proved that the English court has ever bestowed [given] any bribe in this country. For they bestow all offices and pensions; they bribe us, and are masters of us at our own cost, but so long as Scotsmen must go to the English court to obtain offices of trust or profit in this kingdom, those offices will always be managed with regard to the court and interest of England.'

Source 3.10 is a letter from the Duke of Queensberry, the Queen's Commissioner in Scotland. It makes it clear to everyone that they would receive no rewards if they were to vote against the Union. Queensberry was rewarded with an English dukedom and an annual pension of £3000 for his role in supporting the Union.

Source 3.10

Letter from the Duke of Queensberry:

'We were obliged to let it be known that the King was resolved that no man that opposed him should enjoy either place or pension.'

John Campbell, 2nd Duke of Argyll, wrote Source 3.11. He received a military promotion to a major-generalship for his support of the Union and even secured an earldom for his brother.

Source 3.11

John Campbell wrote:

'My Lord, it is surprising to me that my Lord Treasurer, who is a man of sense, should think of sending me up and down like a footman from one country to another without ever offering me any reward. I shall pay the Queen as faithfully as any body can do; but if her ministers think to employ me any further I do think the proposal should be treated with an offer of reward.'

The distribution of pensions, jobs, promotions and money did occur, but they were given to those who were already supporters, or likely to be supporters, of a full Union. Such individuals, however, still expected to be rewarded. Clerk of Penicuik, one of the Scottish Commissioners who negotiated the original Union terms, was made Baron of the Scottish Court of Exchequer. This allowed a comfortable lifestyle for the rest of his life. Clerk was a consistent supporter of Union, hence his appointment as a Scottish Commissioner.

Source 3.12 is a letter written about Seton of Pitmedden in 1704 by a government official. Pitmedden supported Union, but he clearly intended to benefit from his loyalty by getting a good pension.

Source 3.12

Extract from a letter written about Seton of Pitmedden in 1704:

'[Seton of] Pitmedden pretends a great [kindness] to your Lord and says most seriously to me that if your Lord will obtain him a pension of one hundred pounds per annum, he will be your servant and give you a suitable return.'

There are very few examples of anyone receiving a reward and then changing how they voted in the Union debate. George Ogilvy, Lord Banff, is one exception. He went to the final Scottish Parliament to support the Union after he had been given 11 pounds and two shillings (£122 in Scots money). This meant that he agreed to give up his Catholicism during the Parliament; otherwise he would have been prevented from attending because of his religion.

The modern historian Professor Whatley believes that the role of bribery in the Union debate is 'a bit of a red herring actually'. Thirteen Court Party members voted for the Union but received no type of reward at all.

Perhaps one of the best ways of thinking about bribery in the Union debate is provided by the modern historian D. Daiches in Source 3.13.

Put simply, the English court made sure that the likely voters for Union were rewarded. Bribery did not decide the fate of the Union, but political management played an important role.

Was intimidation used as a type of bribery during the Union debate?

In Chapter 2 you learned about the large English armies on the border between Scotland and England and in Ireland during the Union debate in the Scottish Parliament. This could be considered military intimidation because if the Scots rejected Union then an English military invasion was possible.

Source 3.13

D. Daiches writes:

'… pressures of every kind [were] brought to bear by agents of the Government. These pressures, which do not seem to have amounted to outright bribery but in some respects fell little short of it, amounted to a highly successful exercise in political jobbery.'

Source 3.14

Written by a London government official in a letter dated 26 November 1706:

'The troops on the Borders are three regiments of foot, and in the North of Ireland, three of horse, one of foot, and one of dragoons, and they have the necessary orders; but all relating to this affair must be kept very private.'

There was also the threat of the Alien Act of 1705 being reintroduced if Union was not approved by the Scots. This would have ruined Scottish trade with England. Military and economic intimidation were used by the crown and English government ministers during the Union debate, but not all historians would agree that this encouraged members of the last Scottish Parliament to vote for Union in 1707.

Activity

1. You are confronted by Robert Burns who believed that the MPs in the last Scottish Parliament voted for Union because they were 'bought and sold for English gold'. What arguments would you use to counter his beliefs about bribery?

The Articles of Union

The Duke of Hamilton was the leader of the opposition to a full Union. On 1 September 1705, he agreed that Queen Anne should be allowed to appoint the 31 Scottish Commissioners. Opponents of Union reacted with disbelief. A vote in the Scottish Parliament approved this because many of the opponents of Union had already left for their evening meal. The deadlock that had existed since the Scottish Parliament met on 28 June 1705 was ended and negotiations for a full Union began.

The Alien Act 1705 had threatened to ruin Scottish exports with England and treat all Scots in England as foreigners. It was repealed at Westminster in late December 1705. With this threat ended, the Scottish and English Commissioners met in London between 16 April and 11 July 1706.

Most of the Scottish Commissioners were drawn from the Court Party, with connections to either the Duke of Queensberry or the Duke of Argyll. They were joined by members of the Squadrone Volante. Lockhart of Carnwath was the only Jacobite Scottish Commissioner and the only opponent of a full incorporating Union. Lockhart and Clerk of Penicuik, who was also a Scottish Commissioner, wrote that only a full incorporating Union was the likely outcome because the English would not accept a federal Union. The Scottish Commissioners were dominated by members of the landed class. This was to have a dramatic effect on the terms of Union about Scottish commerce (trade).

The two groups of Commissioners met in a London government building and sat in separate rooms. Written statements of their thoughts about each Article of Union were passed between the rooms. There were many smaller meetings between leading Commissioners on both sides but all of the Scottish and English Commissioners never met together in any one meeting. Lockhart left the negotiations early and returned to Scotland because he had been excluded from what he saw as key meetings.

There is a major difference of opinion between leading modern historians about the Commissioners' negotiations. Professor Whatley draws on the writings of Clerk of Penicuik, who says that the meetings were 'convivial' (friendly). Whatley argues that the terms agreed were a good deal for Scotland and show that the Scottish Commissioners were not acting selfishly. On the other hand, Professor Macinnes argues that 'the leading players in the Court Party did not necessarily cut the best deal for Scotland' (Macinness, 2007). The agreed terms of Union were presented to Queen Anne on 23 July 1706.

Source 3.15

An engraving which shows the Treaty of Union being presented to Queen Anne

Source 3.16

An aerial photograph of the area around the old Scottish Parliament

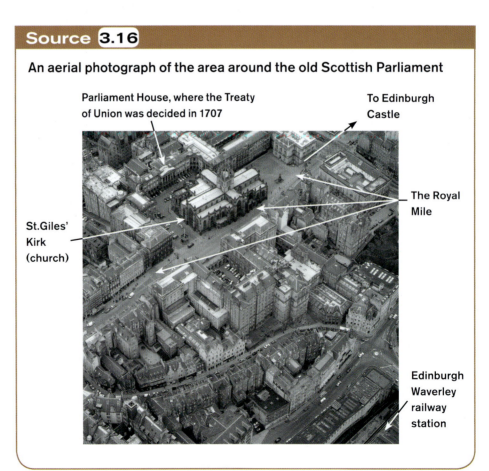

- Parliament House, where the Treaty of Union was decided in 1707
- To Edinburgh Castle
- The Royal Mile
- St. Giles' Kirk (church)
- Edinburgh Waverley railway station

The next step was to get the approval of the Scottish Parliament.

Source 3.17 shows inside Parliament House where the debate over the Treaty of Union took place. After the Scottish Parliament ended, it was used by Scotland's highest law court, the Court of Session.

Source 3.17

Parliament House

The Scottish Parliament met to discuss the terms of the Treaty of Union in October 1706. By late November only four of the 25 Articles of Union had been approved. This was the result of endless debate and delaying tactics by the opposition to Union. In early December, the leading English Government minister, the Earl of Godolphin, authorised the Duke of Queensberry to allow changes to the Articles of Union being debated in the Scottish Parliament. These changes were to be 'indispensable for your majority and not extremely essential to us here in England' (Quoted on www.parliament.uk/actofunion/05_01_edinburgh.html). This created the impression that the terms of Union were fair because the Scots had been allowed to make amendments.

On 16 January 1707, the Treaty of Union, consisting of 25 Articles (terms), was approved by 110 to 68 votes. The Scottish Parliament dissolved on 28 April 1707. The Earl of Seafield remarked 'Now there's ane end to an auld sang'. He was comparing the end of the Scottish Parliament to the end of an old song. This was the same day as 31 dead whales appeared on Kirkcaldy beach. Some people thought that this was a bad sign. On 1 May 1707 the British Parliament met for the first time.

The Treaty of Union 1689–1740

Source 3.18

This is a copy of the Treaty of Union from 7 March 1707

The 25 Articles of Union spoke about the succession, trade, taxation, the Equivalent, privileges, the law and the Scottish crown jewels.

The 25 Articles of Union 1707

The words in red show the alterations (amendments) that the Scots made to the Treaty terms during their debate in the last Scottish Parliament.

Article 1	From 1 May 1707 Scotland and England were united into one kingdom, called Great Britain. The flags of St. Andrew and St. George were combined into one. This made the Union Jack.
Article 2	The succession was to pass to the Protestant House of Hanover. No Catholic or anyone marrying a Catholic was allowed to be monarch of Great Britain.
Article 3	Great Britain was to be represented by one Parliament at Westminster in London.
Article 4	Freedom of trade was to exist within Britain and its colonies.

70

Article 5	All Scottish shipping was to be registered and treated as British.
Article 6	All parts of the United Kingdom of Great Britain were to have the same trading regulations, duties and customs (taxes) on exports and imports, unless individuals had been given special exemptions.
Article 7	The same taxes would apply throughout the United Kingdom on alcohol, but in Scotland there was a lower tax rate on beer than in England.
Article 8	All imported foreign salt was to be taxed at the same rate as England. Scottish salt would not be taxed for 7 years. This was a tax exemption. After this time, the Scots would only pay a third of the English rate. Tax exemptions on salt used for preserving fish and meat were guaranteed.
Article 9	Land tax in Scotland was to be 1/40th of that in England.
Article 10	Scotland had exemption from English duties (taxes) on stamped paper, vellum (finer quality paper) and parchment (paper made from sheep or goat skin).
Article 11	Scotland had exemption from a tax on windows. This would be payable from 1 August 1710.
Article 12	Scotland had exemption from a tax on coal. This would be payable from 30 September 1710.
Article 13	Scotland had exemption from the English malt tax which was due from 24 June 1707.
Article 14	Apart from those stated in the Treaty, Scotland was not to pay any other tax imposed by the English Parliament before the Union took effect. Scottish malt (beer) drunk in Scotland would not be taxed during the War of the Spanish Succession. Scotland would fund itself during 1707. The rate of taxes and duties would be the same for the UK in the future, unless the Great Britain Parliament decided to grant exemptions.
Article 15	The Equivalent was paid to Scotland amounting to 398,085 pounds, 10 shillings (50p). This amount is about £26 million in today's money. This was to pay for • the repayment of Scottish public debts • compensation to the investors in the Darien Scheme

- ending the existence of the Company of Scotland trading to Africa and the Indies
- financial losses made because of the changeover from Scottish to English currency.
- the encouragement of coarse wool manufacture for 7 years at a cost of £2000 per annum
- the annual sum of £2000 paid towards encouraging the fishing industry and other manufactures.

Article 16   English coinage was to be used throughout the United Kingdom.

Article 17   English weights and measures were to be used throughout the United Kingdom.

Article 18   Laws about customs, duties and excise were to be the same throughout the UK. All other Scottish laws were to remain as before the Union took effect, but they could be altered in the future by the Parliament of Great Britain.

Article 19   The Scottish legal system, including its courts, was to remain unchanged but could be altered in the future by the Parliament of Great Britain. No sentences decided in Scotland could be interfered with by English courts. Legal cases relating to customs and excise were to be heard in a new Scottish Court of Exchequer with the same powers as that in England. The Privy Council was to remain in Scotland but its continued existence was not guaranteed. Those who were involved in the Scottish legal system had to have better qualifications.

Article 20   Any positions of influence granted before 1707, which could be passed on to descendents, were to remain. The nobles were able to keep their ancient rights.

Article 21   The Royal Burghs of Scotland kept their traditional rights and privileges.

Article 22   Scotland was to receive 45 MPs in the House of Commons and 16 Peers in the House of Lords. The Scottish Parliament was allowed to pass a separate act which decided the election of peers and MPs to the new British Parliament. This would be considered part of the Treaty.

Article 23   Scottish peers had the same rights and privileges as English peers.

Article 24 A Great Seal of the United Kingdom of Great Britain would replace the separate seals of both Scotland and England. The Scottish crown jewels, parliamentary and other official records were to be kept in Scotland.

Article 25 All laws and Acts of the Scottish Parliament not agreeing with the Articles of Union were to end.

During the debate in the Scottish Parliament, there was considerable unrest on the streets of Edinburgh. Source 3.19 is a drawing of a summer house in a garden mansion in the Canongate area of Edinburgh. It was near to the old Parliament House. There are some people who believe a traditional story that part of the signing of the Treaty by the Scottish MPs took place here. This was to avoid any angry reaction to the signing by the Edinburgh mob. The story tells of how the mob discovered where the signing took place and those who had still to sign had to flee. The MPs hid in the cellar of an Edinburgh house and completed the signing. This story may be anti-Union propaganda from 1707.

Source 3.19

Summer House in Regent Murray's Garden

Were the terms of the Treaty of Union a good deal for Scotland?

In 1707, the Scots achieved access to England's American colonies (Article 4) and compensation for Darien (Article 15). In the 1702 negotiations about Union, the Scots could not get the English to agree to both of these. There were also several amendments made to the original draft terms of Union. These alterations were made because of what was said during the Union debate in the Scottish Parliament. These amendments convinced some Scottish politicians that the terms of Union were fair.

The Scottish crown jewels are shown in Source 3.20. They are called the Honours of Scotland. Article 24 of the Treaty of Union allowed them to stay in Scotland. This amendment to the Treaty terms seemed to recognise the importance of Scottish national identity.

Source 3.20

Scotland's crown jewels

Article 1 of Union was passed by the Scottish Parliament on 4 November 1706, but not by as big a majority as the supporters of Union had hoped. As a result, an 'Act for Securing the Protestant Religion and the Presbyterian Church Government' was passed by the Scottish Parliament on 12 November 1706. This was a very important event. The Church of Scotland ended its opposition to the Union and moderate Presbyterians knew that their church and religion would be secure after the Union.

The number of Scottish MPs and peers in the new British Parliament also seemed to be another Scottish success. Scotland was given 45 MPs and 16 peers. This was more than if the calculation had been based upon the wealth of Scotland compared to England. The Scottish MPs who supported the Union believed that they had negotiated good terms.

Were the terms of the Treaty of Union a bad deal for Scotland?

The English Whig politicians, who were the English Government, were surprised the Scots had not negotiated a much tougher deal. The Whigs were one of two political parties in England. The other party was called the Tories.

The Equivalent in Article 15 was not as large or as good a deal as the English Government had been considering in 1705. The Scots failed to realise that they would be paying for the improvement of their main industries, including fishing, linen and wool, out of their own higher customs and excise taxes! There was no extra money made available to help Scottish manufacturing. This was a huge miscalculation by the Scots. It took 20 years for the Equivalent to be paid because the Scots had failed to be specific about how long it should take to be paid. Higher customs and excise charges also made smuggling more common after 1707.

The economic terms of the Union aimed to end Scotland's threat as an international competitor to England. The Scottish Company of Scotland, which had attempted unsuccessfully to establish a colony at Darien, was brought to an end under Article 15 of Union. The English East Indies Company, however, was allowed to continue. This gave the English control and the profit from a vital trading area.

In an age of empires, the biggest profits were to be made from overseas trade. Some historians believe that this was poorly dealt with by the Treaty of Union. The ability of the Scots to have separate trading partnerships with the Dutch was ended by Article 5 of Union. Article 16 ended the ability of the Scots to use Dutch currency in their trading. Article 18 brought taxation on international trade into line with the English. This all made sure that Scotland could no longer pose a threat by trading abroad with whomsoever she pleased.

In the period between the Union being passed and coming into effect on 1 May 1707, huge quantities of wine, brandy, salt and whale bone (for women's underwear) were brought in from abroad by Scottish merchants. The Scots planned to export these goods to England after 1 May. This would avoid the Scots having to pay customs duties. The Scots made a huge £300,000 profit in four months – about £20 million in today's money. However, as you will learn in the next section, the Union did not bring economic prosperity to Scotland.

English interests still dominated in the new British Parliament because the majority of MPs were English. There were 513 English MPs while Scotland had 45 MPs in the House of Commons. This was less than the total number of MPs from the counties of Devon and Cornwall in England. Scotland also had 16 peers able to sit in the House of Lords, but there were 196 English lords.

Article 24 allowed the Great Seal of Scotland to be kept in Scotland, but the Great Seal of England was used to authorise documents from the British Parliament after 1707. Article 19 of the terms of Union offered no guarantee that the English would not interfere in future matters relating to Scottish law, the Scottish Church and local government. All of this happened after 1707.

Articles 20 and 21 allowed traditional privileges to be kept, but they were largely old fashioned and out of date by this time. The interests of the landed class, in the terms of Union as a whole, were given greater importance than that of overseas trade. The landed classes believed that money could be made from the land and manufacturing, but Article 15 did not make enough money available for investment in Scottish manufacturing.

The painting in Source 3.21 shows the moment in 1818 when Sir Walter Scott found the Scottish Crown Jewels hidden in an oak chest. They had been forgotten about. Some historians believe that this reflected the effect of the Union on Scotland as a whole.

Source 3.21

Sir Walter Scott discovering the 'Honours of Scotland'

The Union of 1707 was unpopular and the politicians in the last Scottish Parliament knew this. They decided that there would be no general election in Scotland to elect MPs to the new British Parliament. The amendment in Article 22 was made to prevent the election of too many Jacobites to the first British Parliament.

The English had achieved a full incorporating Union with Scotland in 1707. They thought that this ended the ability of the Scots to pose a military, trading or political threat. In England, the Union was celebrated as a takeover.

Activities

1. Work in pairs. Copy the spider diagram below.

   The Articles of Union 1707 → Article 4 → Positive – gained access to American colonies
   Article 4 → Negative – the English controlled the East Indies trade

   The idea is to add a positive and negative point about as many of the Articles of Union as possible. One is completed for you as an example.

2. Once you have finished your diagram, can you make a judgement about whether the positives or negatives were the most important? What would be your conclusion?

3. Work in pairs. You must be prepared to take questions from the rest of your classmates about the Articles of Union. One of you will answer questions as though you think that the terms of Union were good and the other must answer the same questions believing the terms to have been bad. Decide as a class how you are going to judge the performance of each pair.

4 The Effects of the Union

The Jacobite Rebellion 1715

In 1708 there was a poorly supported, badly planned and unsuccessful Jacobite rising. A French fleet turned back to France after it was chased by English warships and hit bad weather. James VIII (the 'Old Pretender') had caught measles during the voyage and could not take charge of the campaign. By contrast, the 1715 Jacobite rebellion was the largest of all the Jacobite rebellions, including the more famous one in 1745.

How important for Jacobites was loyalty to the House of Stuart in 1715?

The Jacobites thought that only the House of Stuart had the right to rule. In 1702 King William of Orange died from his injuries when his horse tripped and fell over a mole hill. The Jacobites were delighted. They made a drinking toast to the mole! This was to 'The Little Gentleman in Black Velvet'.

The Jacobites did not accept William or his successors, including Queen Anne who reigned from 1702–1714. Under the terms of the English Act of Settlement 1701, she was succeeded by George I from the Protestant House of Hanover, which is in modern-day Germany.

Source 4.1

A painting of George I (1660–1727)

George I reigned from 1714 until 1727. He spoke German and never learned English properly. He eventually died from a heart attack, brought about by diarrhoea after eating too many strawberries! George I married his cousin Sophia in 1682 and they had two daughters. In 1692 George I imprisoned his wife in a castle, until her death in 1726. George I accused her of having an affair with another man. However, he himself had two very ugly mistresses. One of his mistresses was his illegitimate half-sister! The Jacobite song in Source 4.2 makes fun of George I's private life.

This is verse 1 of the Jacobite song 'Came ye o'er frae France?' It was written before the Battle of Sheriffmuir on 13 November 1715. The Jacobites thought that George I's behaviour made him unfit to be king. Jacobite loyalty to the House of Stuart is part of the explanation for supporting the 1715 rebellion.

Why did Jacobite support increase in 1715?

By 1715, the Union had failed to deliver immediate economic prosperity to Scotland. Modern historians, including Professor Whatley and D. Szechi, believe that this caused the Union to be deeply unpopular and made a huge difference to Jacobite support. The Earl of Mar, who led the Jacobite Rebellion in 1715, was aware of the unpopularity of the Union. Source 4.3 describes Mar's claim that the British Parliament was planning more taxation in Scotland.

Source 4.2

Jacobite song:

'Came ye o'er frae France?
Came ye down by London?
Saw ye Geordie Whelps [George I]?
And his bonny woman [ugly mistress]?
Were ye at the place
Called the Kittle Housie [brothel]?
Saw ye Geordie's grace
Riding on a goosie [prostitute]?'

Source 4.3

D. Szechi argues:

'the [British Parliament] designed to lay unsupportable taxes upon the nation [Scotland]: on lands, corn, cattle, meal, malt, horses, sheep [and] even on cocks and hens, and that this was [good] reason to take up arms since otherwise in a very short time the nation should sink under such burdens.'

Only by allowing for the unpopularity of the Union by 1715 can the massive scale of the 1715 Jacobite rebellion be explained. It is estimated that more than 30,000 male Scots, over 12 per cent of the Scottish population, had some involvement in the 1715 rising. Around eight per cent fought for the Jacobites and around four per cent for the Government side.

Source 4.4 describes the size of the Jacobite army in 1715. Compare this to the 5000 men in the 1689 Jacobite rising.

Source 4.4

A.I. Macinnes reports:

'During the 'Fifteen, the national mobilisation for the Jacobite cause… was… around 16,700. The clans [made] up to 70 % of this force and bore the brunt of the fighting among the 10,000 troops who lined up at Sheriffmuir on 13 November [1715].'

The Union's unpopularity by 1715 is clearly shown by the Jacobite flag unfurled at the start of the rising. It carried as one of its mottos 'No Union'.

Who supported the Jacobites in 1715?

Source 4.5 shows a map of who the Highland Clans supported in 1715. Look back at the same map for the 1689 Jacobite Rebellion on page 5. You should notice that support for the Jacobites in 1715 was more widespread.

Source 4.5

Highland Clan support in 1715

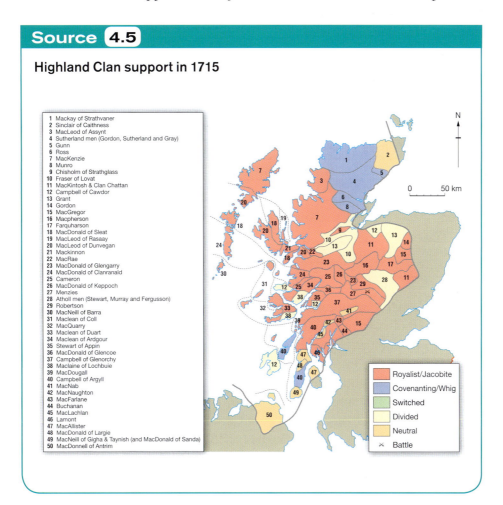

1 Mackay of Strathvaner
2 Sinclair of Caithness
3 MacLeod of Assynt
4 Sutherland men (Gordon, Sutherland and Gray)
5 Gunn
6 Ross
7 MacKenzie
8 Munro
9 Chisholm of Strathglass
10 Fraser of Lovat
11 MacKintosh & Clan Chattan
12 Campbell of Cawdor
13 Grant
14 Gordon
15 MacGregor
16 Macpherson
17 Farquharson
18 MacDonald of Sleat
19 MacLeod of Rasaay
20 MacLeod of Dunvegan
21 Mackinnon
22 MacRae
23 MacDonald of Glengarry
24 MacDonald of Clanranald
25 Cameron
26 MacDonald of Keppoch
27 Menzies
28 Atholl men (Stewart, Murray and Fergusson)
29 Robertson
30 MacNeill of Barra
31 Maclean of Coll
32 MacQuarry
33 Maclean of Duart
34 Maclean of Ardgour
35 Stewart of Appin
36 MacDonald of Glencoe
37 Campbell of Glenorchy
38 Maclaine of Lochbuie
39 MacDougall
40 Campbell of Argyll
41 MacNab
42 MacNaughton
43 MacFarlane
44 Buchanan
45 MacLachlan
46 Lamont
47 MacAllister
48 MacDonald of Largie
49 MacNeill of Gigha & Taynish (and MacDonald of Sanda)
50 MacDonnell of Antrim

Legend: Royalist/Jacobite; Covenanting/Whig; Switched; Divided; Neutral; × Battle

Another difference in 1715 was the support given to the Jacobites by large numbers of Episcopalian landowners and their tenants, who came from the north-east of Scotland. Local ties of loyalty between people were still strong in this area. This is why whole communities in the north-east supported the Jacobites. In the Lowlands, it tended to be individuals and small groups who came out to fight for the Jacobites.

How important was religion for Jacobite supporters in 1715?

The idea that the 1715 Jacobite Rebellion contained only Roman Catholics is incorrect. The table in Source 4.7 shows the religion of the different Highland clans who supported the Jacobites.

Source 4.6

K. M. Brown explains the reasons for Jacobite support:

'Mar [leader of the 1715 rebellion] succeeded in tapping a mixture of genuine Jacobite devotion, Episcopalian frustration, the regional conservatism of the north-east, hatred of the Campbells and political adventuring.'

Source 4.7

Jacobite support and clan religion

	1689–91	1715–16	1745–46
All clans	28	26	18
Episcopalians	14	15	11
Catholics	6	6	4
Presbyterians	0	0	0
Mixed Denominations	8	5	3

Only six Roman Catholic clans supported the 1715 Jacobite Rebellion. Roman Catholics were a minority within Scotland by this time. The majority of Jacobites, from the Highland Clans, the north-east of Scotland and elsewhere, were Episcopalian. The Episcopalians were Protestants but had bishops within their church organisation and rejected the idea of a Presbyterian church dominating Scotland. The Episcopalians were nevertheless willing to accept a Roman Catholic monarch. This explains why the Jacobites, upon seizing Perth on 17 September 1715, proclaimed the Roman Catholic James VIII King of Scotland and shouted 'No Hanoverian!', 'No Popery!', 'No Union!'

It is important, however, not to overemphasise the role of religion in explaining support in the 1715 rebellion. The Union had not had an immediate positive effect on either trade or the amount of money people had and so these issues were still relevant.

Presbyterians who were disappointed with the Union by 1715 did not support the Jacobites. Presbyterians could not support the restoration of a Roman Catholic Stuart to the throne. For those who could not support Jacobitism for religious reasons, their discontent with the Union was shown by their involvement in smuggling.

How important was the use of force in explaining support for Jacobitism in 1715?

The Earl of Mar, who led the Jacobites in 1715, certainly used the threat of force to ensure the support of his tenants for the Jacobite rebellion. This was called 'forcing out'. It is referred to in the letter written by Mar in Source 4.8.

Source 4.8

A letter from the Earl of Mar to John Forbes of Inverernan dated 9 September 1715:

'Let my own tenants in Kildrummy know that if they come not forth with the best arms, that I shall send a party immediately to burn what they shall miss. And they may believe this only a threat, but by all that's sacred, I'll put it into execution, let my loss be what it will, that it may be an example to others. You are to tell the gentlemen that I expect them in their best accoutrements [fighting gear], on horseback and no excuse to be accepted of.'

Forced recruitment is also known to have been used amongst Highland clans, but it must be remembered that the 1715 rebellion began in the middle of the harvest season, when all healthy and fit men were required in the fields. There was some reluctance to go out and fight.

'Forcing out' must, however, be balanced against those clansmen, including the Grants of Glenmoriston and Glenurquhart and the Atholl men, who came out to fight for the Jacobites, despite the wishes of their clan chief.

The size of support for the 1715 rebellion cannot be explained by the use of 'forcing out'.

Why did Jacobite confidence increase by 1715?

Many Scots still had superstitious beliefs in 1715. Reports of unnatural events increased in late 1714 and early 1715, when there was an eclipse of the sun on 22 April.

Source 4.9 is a letter from the Catholic Bishop William Nicolson dated 17 August 1706, in which he described some of the unusual events. Jacobites thought that unusual events were God's way of telling them that a Jacobite rebellion would be successful.

Scottish Jacobites wrongly believed that the English and Welsh Jacobites were about to rebel. They thought this because of street disturbances in English towns, after the English Whigs won the 1714 General Election. The Scottish Jacobites also believed that a rebellion would receive French help. The Earl of Mar, the Jacobite leader in 1715, repeated this belief. French help was unlikely because Louis XVI of France had accepted the Protestant Succession in Britain by signing the Treaty of Utrecht in 1713. The Scottish Jacobites could not have chosen a worse moment to rebel!

> ### Source 4.9
>
> Catholic Bishop William Nicolson's letter, 1706:
>
> 'We are buzzed with prophesies, dreams and visions in a trance, all of the King's return. At least we had rumours of these things, which is enough to keep the people in motion, and some of them I believe well grounded.'

The Scottish Jacobites convinced themselves that the time was right for a rebellion. This was perhaps partly because their friends were made up of other Jacobites. They were also able to organise more effectively than the English Jacobites because the Government knew less about their activities.

Were there selfish reasons for fighting in 1715?

The Jacobite Rebellion in 1715 was led by John Erskine, the Earl of Mar. Mar had lost his government position under George I. On one occasion at the royal court in London, where all the King's ministers and officials gathered, George I turned his back on Mar. When Mar raised the Jacobite standard at Braemar on 9 September 1715, he had little to lose. Mar was nicknamed 'Bobbing John' for having changed sides. It can be argued that Mar rebelled purely for selfish reasons. The modern historian B. Lenman believes that 'Mar's rebellion was really on behalf of the man Mar cared for most in this world – himself' (Lenman,1980).

The unpleasant character of Simon Fraser was on the government side in 1715. He used the 1715 rebellion as the means to be recognised as the 11th Lord Lovat, Chief of the Clan Fraser. He had kidnapped, forcibly married and raped the widowed Lady Lovat of Fraser in 1697.

Source 4.10

B. Lenman describes the marriage ceremony of Simon Fraser to Lady Lovat:

'Pipe music drowned the bride's shrieks while the bridegroom's faithful gillies [attendants] passed the time of the [church] service in thoughtfully slitting Lady Lovat's stays [underwear] with their dirks [daggers].'

William Hogarth was an engraver and artist. He tried to capture the unpleasantness of Simon Fraser in a painting, which is shown in Source 4.11. This was completed shortly before Fraser's execution for his involvement in the 1745 rebellion, but this time on the Jacobite side!

The selfishness displayed by Mar and Fraser was not typical of most who fought in the 1715 Rebellion.

Source 4.11

Simon Fraser, Lord Lovat (1666–1747). How does the artist make Fraser look unpleasant?

How important was hatred of Clan Campbell in explaining Jacobite support in 1715?

In explaining the Jacobite rebellion of 1715, the anti-Campbell element should not be overstated. The Campbells of Glenorchy did, after all, fight for the Jacobites in this rebellion. The modern historian Professor A.I. Macinness explains that being opposed to the Campbells did not automatically mean support for the Jacobites.

Source 4.12

Professor A.I. Maciness states:

'Of the 13 hardcore Jacobite clans in all three risings (1689, 1715, 1745), nine certainly came within the House of Argyll's (Campbells of Argyll) sphere of influence; but another 16 clans also within this sphere of influence were inconsistent in their support of Jacobitism.'

What happened at the Battle of Sheriffmuir 13 November 1715?

Jacobite and Government troops met at Sheriffmuir on 13 November 1715 in the only major battle of the 1715 Rising. The Jacobite army of approximately 10,000 men was around two and a half times the size of the Government army, led by the Duke of Argyll. The left wings of both armies were completely routed (defeated) by the opposing side. The confusion caused by this led to a 30 minute standoff, as the remaining soldiers on both sides watched each other and then left.

Source 4.14 has the words of part of a song, 'The Battle of Sheriffmuir', written after the battle. It shows the confusion which resulted from the battle.

Source 4.13

Map showing the location of the Battle of Sheriffmuir 1715

Source 4.14

Extract from the song 'The Battle of Sherriffmuir':

'There's some say that we wan [won],
Some say that they wan,
And some say that nane [no one] wan ava [at all] man;
There's but ae [one] thing I'm sure,
That at Sheriffmuir,
A battle there was that I saw, man.
And we ran and they ran,
And they ran, and we ran,
And we ran, and they ran awa [away], man.'

The Government and Jacobite forces each claimed victory at Sheriffmuir. Mar had not won because he was an incompetent military commander. He was close to victory because 1000 fresh Jacobite troops were on their way to Sheriffmuir. Mar, however, chose to leave the field!

What happened after the Battle of Sheriffmuir 13 November 1715?

An army of about 1100 Highlanders and 1000 English was defeated at Preston in England on 14 November 1715. Mar had divided his Jacobite army in the weeks before the Battle of Sheriffmuir, in the hope of raising widespread Jacobite support in England. This was another miscalculation by Mar.

James VIII (the 'Old Pretender') only arrived in Scotland at Peterhead on 22 December 1715 in bad health and without any French military support. His arrival is portrayed by a modern artist in Source 4.15.

Source 4.15

In what ways does the artist show James VIII as a pitiful figure?

Any last hopes of victory ended when the ship carrying the Spanish gold to pay for a continuing Jacobite rebellion became stuck on the Dundee sandbanks. The Duke of Argyll's Government army was supported by the Royal Navy and reinforced with the arrival of 6000 Dutch and Swiss troops in December 1715. On 4 February 1716, James left Montrose for France, accompanied by Mar.

Source 4.16

The modern historian D. Szechi concludes that:

'... the '15 was also one of the most incompetently conducted, half cocked, botched-up jobs ever set in motion by a group of plotters throughout the long 18th Century...'

Activities

1. In a group of three make a list of the reasons for the 1715 Jacobite Rebellion. Use the flow chart below to help you. Allocate a percentage to each of your reasons to show its importance. You may want to read pages 92–105 on the Effects of Union before deciding your percentages.

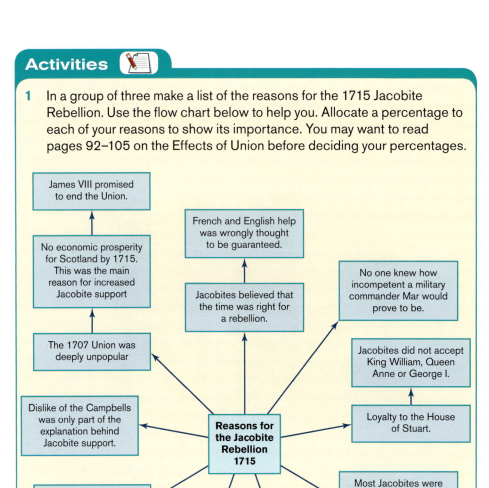

2. Convert your percentages into a pie chart to form either a large (A3) poster or computer presentation. Present your pie chart to the rest of your class. Each member of the group should take it in turn to explain and justify the sections of your pie chart. If you have all understood this issue, there should be no great differences between the pie charts from different groups.

The Jacobite Rebellion 1719

After the failure of the 1715 rebellion some Jacobites fled to France and into exile. In Scotland, every effort was made to avoid government revenge being taken on known Jacobites. There were approximately 40 executions in England but only one in Scotland. There was also widespread opposition to any attempt to try Scottish prisoners in England and Scottish lawyers delayed attempts to forfeit (confiscate) Jacobite estates. There was a genuine attempt to restore normal life in Scotland after the 1715 rebellion. This approach helps to explain the reduced support for both the 1719 and 1745 Jacobite rebellions.

In 1719, the Spanish supported another Jacobite rebellion. They sent 27 ships and about 7000 men in the main fleet from Spain. This fleet was to land in England but was destroyed in a storm. The survivors returned to Spain. Only two ships and 300 Spanish soldiers made it to Scotland. This was a diversionary force and not part of the main fleet. The Spanish wanted to divert English attention and resources away from their war in Europe. The War of the Spanish Succession had ended in 1714, but England and Spain were again at war after 1717 over the control of territory in Europe.

The arrival of the Spanish in Scotland received limited Highland support. The failure of the Spanish to bring a large number of soldiers probably had a lot to do with this. William MacKenzie, the 5th Earl of Seaforth, was the leading Highland Jacobite. His stronghold was Eilean Donan Castle on Loch Duich in Wester Ross, which you can see in Source 4.17.

Source 4.17

Eilean Donan Castle as it is today, after being rebuilt by 1932. The castle was destroyed in 1719, firstly by gunfire from three English warships and then by 27 barrels of gunpowder, which blew it up after capture

The 1719 rising attracted no more than 1000 Jacobites but the leadership was divided. Without the support from the shipwrecked main Spanish fleet, it had little chance of success. A battle was fought at Glenshiel on 10 June 1719, near to Eilean Donan Castle, which the Government army won. Although the Government army was the same size as the Jacobites, it had the advantage of artillery. Jacobite casualties were higher than those of the Government army as a result.

The painting of The Battle of Glenshiel in Source 4.18 shows the battle in progress. It is thought to have been based upon a drawing made by someone who fought in the battle. A hill near to the scene of the battle is called The Coirein nan Spainteach (The Pass of Spaniards) because the Spanish soldiers fled over it. They later surrendered and were eventually allowed to return to Spain. There was no further Jacobite rebellion until 1745.

Source 4.18

The Battle of Glenshiel, 1719

The Effects of Union by 1740

What was the immediate effect of the Union?

There was no immediate economic prosperity brought to Scotland by the Union of 1707.

Source 4.19

M. Lynch describes the limited effects of Union:

'Few historians would dispute that economic benefits did not materialise before the 1740s, and even then they came only in specific sectors of the economy, such as linen, coarse woollen cloth and black cattle. The worst forecasts of the swamping of Scottish manufactures after 1707 did not happen but such industries found at best only sluggish demand for their products in the new English market, both domestic and colonial. In the most important sector of the Scottish economy, in which eight or nine out of every ten Scots were still employed – in agriculture – the effects were marginal.'

The Union encouraged a rapid growth in smuggling to avoid increased customs duties. These taxes were five times higher after 1707. In the early period after Union, almost one quarter of tobacco imports from the

American colonies were probably smuggled. Between 1715 and 1717 around 62 per cent of all imported goods into Scotland were smuggled! This was a remarkable level of smuggling.

Source 4.20

Auchmithie harbour

Source 4.20 is a photograph of Auchmithie harbour near Arbroath in the north-east of Scotland. This area had a reputation for smuggling after 1707. Fishing boats would be used to hide items such as tobacco and brandy, which would be brought ashore, sometimes during the night or inside fish. The coastline of Scotland was ideal for smuggling.

There were more customs and excise men after 1707, but the amount of taxation collected decreased. Robert Burns, the famous Scottish poet, titled one of his poems 'The Deil's Awa Wi' Th' Exciseman'. In this poem, the people were delighted when the devil took away the exciseman (taxman)!

In Scotland after 1707, there were riots and attacks on excise men and their warehouses, which stored captured smuggled goods. During March 1714 a customs officer in Ayr was attacked with blocks of ice and stones. In 1722, soldiers had to defend the customs warehouse at Perth. Attempts to collect the 1725 Malt Tax led to the Shawfield Riot in Glasgow. This also sparked riots in Paisley, Stirling, Dundee, Ayr and Elgin. There was a riot in Fraserburgh in 1735 because the excise men searched local houses for smuggled brandy while the people attended church.

Wages and living standards remained low until the 1760s. This made smugglers into heroes.

Source 4.21

An engraving entitled 'The Porteous Mob, AD 1736', by James Drummond, 1862. It shows the Edinburgh mob searching for Captain Porteous who had executed a smuggler and shot and killed people in the crowd.

The Reverend Alexander Carlyle's account in Source 4.22 describes the Porteous Riot in Edinburgh on 14 April 1736. Carlyle witnessed the riot as a schoolboy. He suggested that there was widespread sympathy in Scotland for the smugglers and those who murdered Porteous and hung his body on a pole.

Source 4.22

Reverend Alexander Carlyle's account of the Porteous Riot in 1736:

'Soon after the executioner had done his duty, there was an attack made upon him, as usual on such occasions, by the boys and blackguards [ruffians] throwing stones and dirt [at] the hangman. But there was no attempt to break through the guard and cut down the prisoner. There was very little, if any, more violence than had usually happened on such occasions. Porteous (Captain of Edinburgh City Guard), however, inflamed with wine and jealousy, thought proper to order his Guard to fire, their muskets loaded with slugs. They obeyed, and fired; but wishing to do as little harm as possible, many of them elevated their pieces [guns], the effect of which was that some people were wounded in the windows; and one unfortunate lad, whom we had displaced, was killed in the stair window by a slug entering his head. We had seen many people, women and men, fall on the street. We saw the lying dead or

Source 4.22 continued

wounded. The numbers were said to be eight or nine killed, and double the number wounded; but this was never exactly known. Porteous was tried and condemned to be hanged, but he was reprieved [given a royal pardon which set him free] [and] removed to the Castle for greater security. But a plot was laid and conducted by some persons unknown with the greatest secrecy forcing the prison the night before, and executing the sentence upon him themselves with no interruption, though there were five companies of a marching regiment lying in the Canongate [an area of Edinburgh].'

No one was convicted of murder against Porteous. Scottish MPs in the House of Commons and Scottish churchmen opposed severe punishment for those responsible. Widespread smuggling was evidence of disappointment with the effects of the Union.

What effect did the 1707 Union have on Scottish industries?

A number of Scottish industries were badly hit by the effects of the Union. Professor A. Macinnes believes that Scotland suffered an economic recession until the middle of the eighteenth century because she was the weaker partner in the Union of 1707.

Wool exports were banned after the Union and Scottish manufacturers struggled to compete with better quality and cheaper English cloth. Linen was perhaps the worst hit. Scottish linen was poor quality. In 1711, the British Parliament imposed further export duties on linen. Only the English linen industry was allowed to claim back tax on soap in 1714. There was a huge market for the sale of linen cloth to the American colonies. This was used to clothe the

Source 4.23

Daniel Defoe's 'The Aftermath of the Union of Parliaments 1723':

'I take the decay of all these seaports which 'tis evident have made a much better figure in former times…
It is true, the reason is in part evident, namely, poverty: no money to build vessels, hire seamen, buy nets and materials for fishing, to cure [salt] the fish when it is caught, or carry it to market when it is cured. People tell us, that slothfulness [laziness] bets [brings] poverty, and that is true; but I must add too, that poverty makes slothfulness, and I doubt not, were two or three merchants to settle at Kirkubry, who had stock to furnish out ships and boats for these things, they would soon find the people as industrious, as in other places.
In a word, the common people all over the country, not only are poor, but look poor; they appear dejected, and discouraged, as if they had given over all hopes of ever being otherwise than what they are.'

many slaves who grew cotton on the plantations. The Scottish linen industry took decades to benefit from this because it lacked investment.

A tax was put on salt exports in 1711. It caused riots in Dumfries and Galloway because salt was an everyday item used in porridge, oatcakes and preserving fish. In May 1713 a Malt Tax was introduced. This broke Article 13 of Union and led directly to the 1713 vote in the House of Lords to try to dissolve the Union.

Brewing, papermaking, east-coast fishing (because of higher taxes on imported salt), Forfar shoe-making and Dundee candle-making were amongst other industries badly affected by the Union.

Daniel Defoe travelled through Scotland after the Union. He was forced to concede that the effects of Union had not been as positive as he had expected. Defoe describes Kirkcudbright in 1723 in Source 4.23.

The British Government was not interested in the Scottish economy until the 1720s but even then there were only nine acts passed by the British Parliament between 1727–45 which dealt with Scotland.

Source 4.24

Professor A.I. Macinnes believes that the Board of Trustees was set up by the British Government in 1727 to encourage industry in Scotland as a means to prevent further unrest:

'Indeed, it can be contended that [government] development funds and bounties [rewards] were primarily forthcoming because of the fear that Jacobite unrest would capitalise on the Shawfield Riots against the malt tax in Glasgow in 1725 and the Porteous Riots against the execution of smugglers in Edinburgh in 1736.'

In Source 4.25 the modern historian M. Lynch argues that the British Government wanted to keep Scotland under control. After 1725, the most important manager of government affairs in Scotland was Archibald Campbell, Earl of Islay.

Source 4.25

M. Lynch writes:

'London was interested in Scotland only when it proved troublesome… Scotland was run by managers, who were expected to keep Scottish MPs and peers in line… and to hold Scotland itself quiet.'

What was the effect of Union on the Highlands of Scotland?

The Union of 1707 aimed to end the Jacobite threat which came from the Highlands. This explains the appearance of the Society in Scotland for Propagating Christian Knowledge in 1709. It aimed to promote

Presbyterianism and English-speaking education in the Highlands and Islands. This meant replacing the Episcopalian and Catholic religions and the Gaelic language.

Six government regiments were founded in the Highlands after 1707 to keep order and enforce the Disarming Acts of 1716 and 1725. In 1739 they became the Black Watch Regiment with a dark green/black tartan plaid (traditional highland clothing). This colour gave the regiment their name and was probably chosen as a means of camouflage. Source 4.26 shows another example of highland plaid.

There was also a huge military road-building programme of over 250 miles in the Highlands. General George Wade was in charge of this. Fort William and Fort George were renovated and Fort Augustus built.

Source 4.26

Highland plaid

Source 4.27

General Wade's bridge at Aberfeldy, Perthshire

All this was meant to keep the Jacobite threat quiet, but it did nothing to help manufacturing in the Highlands. In the 1745 rebellion, the Jacobites used the new roads to move their soldiers! The same roads were later used by the people to emigrate.

Source 4.28

Fort George near Inverness

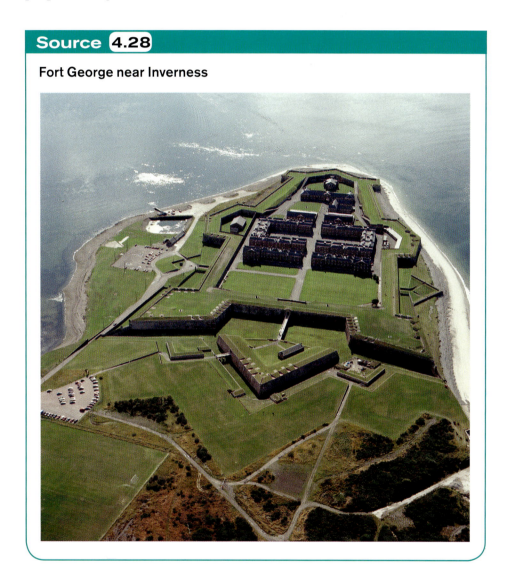

Traditional Highland society was based upon the chief and his clan. It had not used money to any great extent. This had started to change with the growth of the black cattle trade before 1707. Highland cattle were taken to Lowland Scotland and England before 1707 to feed the growing town populations. This trend continued after 1707.

Source 4.29

Black cattle

The highest road in Britain is the road to Applecross in Wester Ross and is called the Pass of the Cattle (Bealach na Ba) because it was built upon an old drove road. These drove roads were used to take black cattle to the lowland markets.

Watch these two videos entries for a journey up the Bealach na Ba:
www.youtube.com/watch?v=QDsmU6v2Egg
www.youtube.com/watch?v=rubzQiWrS5g

Falkirk and Crieff were the trysts (markets) where black cattle from the Highlands and Islands went to be auctioned and fattened before continuing south.

The Gaelic poets expressed their concern at the growing debts of the Highland chiefs because of their expensive lifestyles. In the 1730s, the clan chief Macleod of Dunvegan tried to sell some of his clansmen into the American colonies as slaves, where they would grow cotton.

Source 4.30

The drove roads taken by the cattle to market

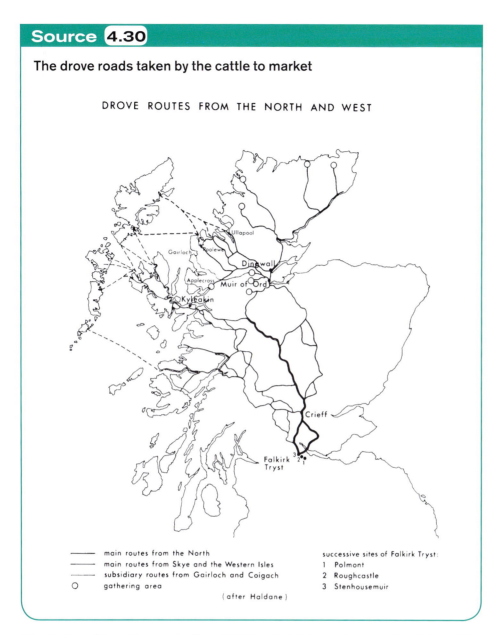

DROVE ROUTES FROM THE NORTH AND WEST

— main routes from the North
— main routes from Skye and the Western Isles
— subsidiary routes from Gairloch and Coigach
○ gathering area

successive sites of Falkirk Tryst:
1 Polmont
2 Roughcastle
3 Stenhousemuir

(after Haldane)

The Duke of Argyll was the first Highland chief to take away land from his clan and rent it out to any one person who offered the most money. He did this in Morvern and on the islands of Mull and Tiree in the 1730s. The people who were already on the land were moved elsewhere. The old custom had been to rent the land to the chief's clansmen. The rent, however, could be paid in crops or labour.

The Duke of Argyll's decision served as a model for the later Highland Clearances in the second half of the eighteenth century, when other chiefs did the same. The people were replaced with sheep because sheep were worth more money. The failure of the Jacobite Rebellion in 1745–6 ended any sense of loyalty by many of the chiefs towards their clan. Mass eviction and emigration followed.

The harshness and poverty of Highland life after the Union is captured in the letters written by Edmund Burt, who spent most of his time in and around Inverness after being sent there to work as a government contractor in 1730. Edmund Burt drew the illustration of fishermen being carried back to shore by their women near Inverness (Source 4.31). There was no proper landing area for the small boats!

Edmund Burt also wrote Source 4.32 about the people in the Inverness area in 1730.

Source 4.31

Edmund Burt's illustration of fishermen near Inverness

Source 4.32

Edmund Burt reported:

'I have seen women by the riverside washing parsnips, turnips, and herbs, in tubs, with their feet. An English lieutenant-colonel told me, that about a mile from the town he saw, at some little distance, a wench [young woman] turning and twisting herself about as she stood in a little tub; and as he could perceive, being on horseback, that there was no water in it, he rode up close to her, and found she was grinding off the beards and hulls of barley with her naked feet, which barley, she said, was to make broth [soup] and, since that, upon inquiry, I have been told it is a common thing.
They hardly ever wear shoes. I have seen some of them come out of doors, early in a morning, with their legs covered up to the calf with dried dirt, the remains of what they contracted in the streets the day before.'

The Union of 1707 did not provide investment for the Highland economy and there was still sympathy for the Jacobites in many areas.

Were moderate Presbyterians pleased with the effects of Union?

Moderate Presbyterians were key supporters of the Union in 1707. They thought that the Union guaranteed their religion from any future threat but they were disappointed by events after 1707.

James Greenshields was an Episcopalian minister who was put in prison because he held church services in Edinburgh. He appealed to the House of Lords in London, which reversed the Scottish decision. In 1712, The Toleration Act granted Episcopalians the right to worship in public, while the Patronage Act gave landowners the right to appoint local ministers. This meant that Episcopalian landowners could appoint Presbyterian ministers. This prevented local Presbyterians choosing their own minister.

Scottish Presbyterians were also annoyed by the Yule Vacance Act. This recognised Christmas as a holiday in the Scottish law courts. This was against Presbyterian beliefs. Presbyterians thought that Christmas was a pagan (non-Christian) and Catholic festival. When the right to publish the Bible in Scotland passed to a new printing company that employed a Catholic and Episcopalians, Presbyterians were outraged.

How did the Scottish political elite react to the effects of the 1707 Union?

The Scottish political elite had many reasons for being disappointed with the immediate effects of the Union. The Duke of Hamilton had been rewarded with a British peerage, the Duke of Brandon, but he was refused the right to sit in the House of Lords.

In February 1708 the Privy Council was abolished. The Privy Council was not guaranteed by the Articles of Union, but it did appear to be a breach of the spirit behind the terms of Union.

The same seemed to be true of the Equivalent because it took 20 years for it to be fully paid. The first payment of the Equivalent arrived with a significant amount in paper money. The Scots were suspicious of this and the Edinburgh mob stoned those who delivered the money chest.

The 1707 Union did not guarantee Scots law. The much harsher English Law of Treason was implemented in Scotland in 1708 after the Jacobite rebellion. This caused outrage even amongst non-Jacobites.

The new Scottish Court of Exchequer was responsible for customs and excise but it followed an English model. An English judge was in charge. One of the four judges was also English throughout the eighteenth century. This was a positive thing because it gave the Scots experience of laws relating to trade and business, but it shows that one of the Treaty of Union's key aims was to protect English trading interests.

As members of the British Parliament, Clerk of Penicuik describes in Source 4.33 how the Scots were made to feel unwelcome when they arrived in London after 1707.

Three leading supporters of Union in 1707, the Earls of Seafield and Mar, along with the Duke of Argyll, proposed a bill to the House of Lords on 1 June 1713 to dissolve the Union. It failed by only four votes.

Were there Scots who benefited from the Union of 1707?

There were individual Scots who benefited from the Union between 1707 and 1740 as the British Empire grew. Scots took half of all land grants over 100 acres on the Caribbean island of St. Kitts. One half of all the medical men on the Caribbean island of Antigua were Scots by 1731. The Scots doctor William Hamilton cured the Indian Emperor of venereal disease (VD). There were also successful lowland tobacco lords trading with the American colonies and Highland chiefs involved in the black cattle trade.

Source 4.33

From Clerk of Penicuik, writing in 1730:

'[Scottish MPs were] obscure and unhonoured in the crowd of English society and the unfamiliar intrigues of English politics, where they were despised for their poverty, ridiculed for their speech, sneered at for their manners, and ignored in spite of their votes by the ministers and government.'

Source 4.34

A modern artist's impression of wealthy tobacco lords

Landlords, farmers and merchants were able to export large amounts of grain in the first 15 years after Union because of Article 15 of the Union. This did, however, lead to ordinary people fearing grain shortages. In the south-west of Scotland some people lost land for black cattle pens to be made. This land was used to fatten the Highland cattle before they continued south.

> **Source 4.35**
>
> M. Lynch believes:
>
> '… although there were many improvers, there was comparatively little improvement – until economic circumstances made it profitable in the last two decades of the 18th Century.'

Some landowners, including John Cockburn of Ormiston and Sir Archibald Grant of Monymusk, also experimented with new forms of agriculture. Cockburn went bankrupt and had to sell his estate. The modern historian M. Lynch argues in Source 4.35 that agricultural improvement was limited.

The British Government took an interest in helping the Scottish economy in the 1720s because the Union was proving so unpopular. By 1740, the British Empire, through its colonies, foreign wars and possibilities for manufacturing, created opportunities for individual Scots, but not necessarily Scotland.

The table on the following page provides a useful summary of how the Treaty of Union addressed the concerns of Scots in theory, though in practice problems still remained.

The Treaty of Union 1689–1740

Concern before 1707	Article addressing concern	Remaining problem after 1707
succession and security	Article 2	Jacobite Rebellions 1708, 1715, 1719
access to American Colonies and free trade	Article 4	Scots excluded from East Indies trade; smuggling increased and included the American colonies; Scotland experienced economic recession after 1707
Darien and the question of compensation	Article 15	It took 20 years for the Equivalent to be paid; the Equivalent amount was not as good as in the 1705 proposal; not enough money for investment in Scottish manufacturing
taxation	Article 6, 7, 8, 13, 14	customs and exercise duties increased; smuggling increased; riots increased
religion and Presbyterianism	a separate act guaranteed Presbyterianism	Presbyterianism upset by Toleration Act, Patronage Act, Yule Vacance Act, and who had the right to publish the bible
Scottish Law	Article 19	Scottish court decisions referred to House of Lords; Privy Council abolished
the number of Scottish MPs and Peers	Article 22	Scottish MPs had little influence in the British Parliament
Scottish identity	Article 24	Scottish crown jewels locked away and forgotten about; English Great Seal used for documents; Scottish MPs made to feel unwelcome in London

Activity

1   Your challenge is to produce a display or presentation. This will be divided into two parts: the first part of your display will show Scotland before 1707; the second part of your display will show the main effects of the Union on Scotland by 1740 as they apply to your course of study. Your display or presentation must make people want to stop and look at your views about the impact of the Union on Scotland.

Work in a group of no more than four. Your teacher will give you an appropriate time scale. Your display or presentation should deal with the following topics for Scotland before 1707 and Scotland in 1740:

- Scotland's identity
- Scotland's economy

continued

104

Activities continued

- Scotland's politics
- how religion affected attitudes to Union
- the Scottish Highlands.

Remember, you will have to look back at earlier chapters. Your display must be visible across a classroom. Your display must use at least three colours and must use at least two sizes of text. Think creatively – who said it has to be paper based?

Somewhere in your display or presentation each topic should have:

- a four sentence text box explaining your ideas
- one illustration – or two if you want to show differing points of view
- a smart slogan summarising the core issue associated with the topic.

Looking Back on the Union

Why was the Treaty of Union passed?

Historians do not agree about the reasons explaining why the Treaty of Union was passed in 1707. This book has argued that understanding the problems created by an age of empires is a key factor in explaining why the Union of 1707 came about. The table below gives a summary of some of the different explanations offered by historians.

Historian	Key idea explaining the Union
P.H. Scott and W. Ferguson	Leading Scottish politicians were bribed and gave in to English military intimidation.
P.H. Brown	Scotland was only able to develop as a modern state by agreeing to a full Union. Scotland was too poor to survive on her own. Union with England was the only option. England was willing to help Scotland.
P. Riley	Union resulted from a power struggle between rival groups within the Scottish landowning elite. The winners knew that they would control Scotland. This would give them the benefit of government positions and salaries.
T.C. Smout	Scotland was in a dreadful economic condition. Union with England was the only way to improve the Scottish economy.
C. Whatley	The Scottish economy was in a bad way and Scottish Presbyterianism needed to be protected against the Jacobites. Scottish politicians had principles and were not bribed. The Treaty of Union was a good deal for Scotland.
A.I. Macinnes	The English empire was growing and needed Scottish resources. The terms of Union could have been much better. The Scots believed the Scottish economy to be weaker than it really was. They did not understand the strengths of Scotland's overseas trade. Queen Anne protected her royal powers by getting a full Union passed. Supporters of Union wanted to end the Jacobite threat. The Union served English interests and not Scottish ones first and foremost.

If you go to www.youtube.com/watch?v=KdRSJJPXKIs you will see a trailer for a newly released computer game set in 1701. It is based upon the idea of an age of empires and the wars which resulted between the great powers.

Source 5.1

M. Fry further develops the theory about the problems created for smaller states in an age of empires:

'The union with Scotland formed Great Britain, which was the foundation of the modern United Kingdom, and in particular of the Empire. As a prelude [start] to empire and to the great economic expansion of Victorian times, and to Britain as an enormous trading power, England had to come to terms in some fashion with the other nations occupying the [island]. Without that the rest would not have been possible. Just as France had to subdue everything to the West of the Rhine, and Spain had to end the autonomy [independence] of the kingdoms which had first constituted [made up] the Spanish monarchy, and as Russia had to expand to the Baltic and the Austrian empire had to expand into central Europe, so for England, a sine quo none [requirement] of its future imperial status was to come to terms in some way with the other nations occupying the archipelago [island].'

The English and, after 1707, British Empire is estimated to have spent more than £100 million sterling between 1689 and 1713 on its increasingly costly foreign wars. Between 1648 and 1713, there were 22 wars in Europe. The English/British Empire was based upon debt, whereas the French Empire relied upon plunder.

In 1707, England's national debt was about £14.5 million. By 1714 it had risen to £36 million. This has led some historians to argue that the English had taken over Scotland as part of their plan to grow the English Empire. This idea is suggested by three modern historians in Sources 5.2, 5.3 and 5.4 and a modern television presenter and author in Source 5.5.

Source 5.2

Professor N. Ferguson writes:

'The United Kingdom of Great Britain and Ireland (after 1922 only Northern Ireland)… was and is to all intents and purposes an English empire; for brevity's sake, it is still commonly referred to as England.'

Source 5.3

Professor Whatley argues:

'… there are grounds for suspecting that, by and large, English enthusiasm for the union was "of a firmly imperialist cast".'

The Union happened when it did because Scotland posed a number of specific threats to the continued costly expansion of the English Empire. The first threat was military.

Source 5.4

K.M. Brown suggests:

'union being perceived by many English members of Parliament as a form of conquest.'

Source 5.5

J. Paxman, television presenter and author, states:

'One of the characteristics of the English which has most enraged the other races who occupy their island is their thoughtless readiness to muddle up 'England' with 'Britain'. It is, to listen to some English people talk, as if the Scots and Welsh either did not exist, or were just aspiring to join some master race which has always been in control of its God-ordained destiny. The English would do well to mind their language... it is also true that the British Empire was in large part the creation of Scots...'

The second threat to England from Scotland was political. Queen Anne did not want to have limitations imposed upon the powers of her successors by the Scottish Parliament. The Claim of Right and Articles of Grievance in 1689, the Act of Security and Act Anent Peace and War in 1703, the Wine Act 1703 and Wool Act 1704 clearly showed that the Scottish Parliament could oppose the monarch's authority. A full Union ended the existence of the Scottish Parliament and therefore ended this danger.

Source 5.6

Professor J. Charnley, Head of History, University of East Anglia, writes:

'The function [of the union] in 1707 is superseded [replaced] in many ways. Insofar as it was meant to prevent the French using a hostile Scotland as a base from which to launch a Jacobite rebellion against the Hanoverians, it has no use.'

The third threat to England was over trade. This is called a commercial threat. Scotland had a successful overseas trade with Ireland and Europe. Scotland was particularly successful in trading with the American colonies, but this trade was illegal under the English Navigation Acts. Although it failed, Scotland's ambitions were made clear by the attempt to establish a colony at Darien. Scotland's illegal American trade and the Darien scheme convinced England of the need to control Scottish trade and use it to benefit an English-dominated British Empire. A full Union guaranteed that England would have Scottish manpower for the colonies, manufacturing and her wars. The Union of 1707 was viewed by England as a solution to the problems posed by Scotland.

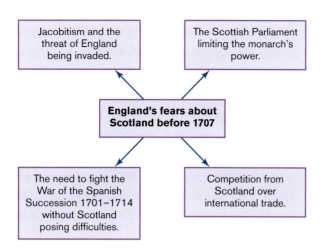

A majority of Scottish politicians in the country's last Parliament supported Union because they believed Scotland's economy to be in a terrible state after recession, famine and the Darien affair. Modern research has shown that the Scottish economy was recovering by 1707 and Darien did not have the disastrous financial effects as previously thought. The same politicians lost confidence in the ability of Scotland to survive without a closer Union with England. This was because they lived in an age of empires, when countries were charging high taxes on the goods of rival countries. This is called protectionism.

Many of the Scottish politicians who supported Union came from the landed classes. They were prepared to accept terms of Union which made Scotland's future economic development depend upon agriculture (landed enterprise) rather than developing overseas trade. Their inexperience in issues of trade explains why several of the terms of Union were incompetent, especially Article 15.

The Scottish politicians who supported Union did have principles and were not merely bribed into voting for Union. They had good reasons to vote for Union but this is not to deny elements of selfishness and the distribution of rewards to Union supporters.

Source 5.7

Professor A.I. Macinnes asserts:

'National independence was sacrificed for the preservation of aristocratic privilege, the institutional autonomy [independence] of the Kirk [Presbyterian Church] and the prospect of economic gain through unfettered [unlimited] access to imperial [colonies] as well as English markets.'

The Scottish supporters of Union genuinely, but mistakenly, thought that they had secured good terms in the final Treaty of Union. Economic and military threats convinced Union supporters that Union was the only possible option.

> ### Source 5.8
>
> Professor A.I. Macinnes argues that the Dutch offered an alternative to full union with England, but they were never asked:
>
> 'Association with England was a more feasible, though not necessarily less bloody or more commercially sound, option than an alliance with the United Provinces [Dutch], at least until Jacobitism was crushed and Empire expanded.'

The Treaty of Union was approved by the Scottish Parliament because the opposition was divided, popular opinion ignored and the Squadrone Volante decided to support Union.

What were the effects of Union?

Historians do not agree about this either! The evidence in this book argues that Scotland entered a recession in the period after Union. The Union of 1707 did nothing to help the weaknesses in the Scottish economy because the terms agreed for investment were inadequate. Individual Scots benefited from Union, but Scotland did not.

> ### Source 5.9
>
> Professor T. Devine writes:
>
> 'The old aphorism [saying], which is crude but broadly correct, that England ruled the empire while the Scots managed it, is broadly speaking at least for the 18th and most of the 19th Century, correct.'

Widespread smuggling and continuing Jacobitism are evidence of how various groups at the time thought the Union was disappointing. Professor A.I. Macinnes stresses in Source 5.10 that the effects of the Union ignored Scottish needs and this gave a boost to Jacobitism.

> ### Source 5.10
>
> Professor A.I. Macinnes states:
>
> 'Successive breeches of the spirit as well as the substance of the treaty, the consequent subordination of Scotland to the dictates [demands] of predominantly English ministries and the monopolising [control] of patronage [rewards] and places of profit by their favoured political managers ensured that Jacobitism remained a viable cause in Scotland.'

Some historians believe that the eighteenth century Enlightenment only happened because of the 1707 Union. This movement was centred in Edinburgh and would shape the ideas about government and society in the modern world. The ideas for this were, however, laid in the Scottish traditions of an earlier age before 1707.

Is the Union important today?

> **Source 5.11**
>
> **A cartoonist's view of what a previous Labour Prime Minister (1997–2007), Tony Blair, really thought about the attempts of nationalists to end the Union**
>
>

The final thoughts in this book about Scotland and the Union of 1707 are provided by two very different modern-day historians. Source 5.12 records the answer of the English historian David Starkey to a question about whether 23 April should be a national holiday in England, in order to celebrate St. George's Day, the patron saint of England.

> **Source 5.12**
>
> **David Starkey speaking on the BBC 1 programme 'Question Time', 23 April 2009:**
>
> 'If we decide to go down this route of an English national day, it will mean that we have become a feeble little country just like the Scots and the Welsh and the Irish. Once upon a time England was a great country. Remember, we [England] are distinguished by the fact we don't have national dress [or a] deeply boring provincial [unimportant] poet [Robert] Burns. We don't have national music like the awful bagpipe. What the Scots and the Welsh are, are typical small nations with a romantic, 19th Century style nationalism.'

Source 5.13

P.H. Scott, a Scottish historian, believes that the Union helped to produce a particular way of thinking in Scotland, with a:

'sense of weariness, of the absence of hope, and of lacerating [wounding] self-contempt [criticism] which is a marked component in the psyche [thinking] of "colonised people".'

As you can see, the debate about Scotland and the Union of 1707 continues to promote strong feelings!

Activities

1. Your target is to teach a lesson, in groups of three or four, to the rest of your class which is linked to the issue of EITHER the causes OR the effects of the Union. Your main resource for information is this textbook but you must also research, find, beg or borrow other resources to make your lesson come alive. Your lesson must show imagination.

   Negotiate with your teacher over how long you have to prepare your lesson. You should present your lesson in an organised, interesting, mature and informative way. Planning is vital – and all in your group must participate. Decide who is going to do what job in the group. Your lesson should last between five and 10 minutes. You must include visual material into your lesson, e.g. PowerPoint or whiteboard elements.

   As in any lesson there are really important things for you to decide and aim for:

   - What do you want your students to be able to do and know at the end of your lesson?
   - How will you assess the success of your lesson – in other words what will you expect to see or hear your students doing to prove your lesson has been successful?

2. It is now time to vote. The year is 1740 and you have the right to decide to vote for or against a full incorporating Union with England having heard the arguments. Work in a group of three or four. Each member of your group must play a different character. The characters are a wealthy landowner (noble), a merchant and a less wealthy landowner (gentry). Ordinary working people in towns and the countryside were not allowed to become members of either the Scottish Parliament before 1707 or British Parliament after 1707. You may choose, however, to have such a person as one of your characters for this exercise. Each of your characters must also choose a religion. Your choices are Presbyterian, Episcopalian and Roman Catholic.

   Discuss in your group how you think each of your characters will vote. You must have reasons for your decision based upon what you have learned in this book and heard in your presentations for Activity 1. Write yes or no on a slip of paper and place it into a voting box. Your teacher will count the result.

continued

Activities continued

3 You must now prepare and give a short explanation to the rest of your class about why you have decided to vote for or against the Union. You must describe the kind of character that you have chosen. Your class members and teacher may challenge your voting decision.

Preparing for Paper 2 of the Higher History Exam

Paper 2 of your Higher History exam is based entirely on source analysis. The exam paper will be divided into five special topics. This book is about ONE of those special topics: The Treaty of Union 1689–1740.

What will Paper 2 of my exam be about?

You only have to answer ONE special topic section. You must answer the questions set on the special topic you have studied.

There will be questions on other special topics that other candidates have studied. Make sure you answer the correct special topic.

Your special topic syllabus is divided into six main issues. Check out the Arrangements document on the SQA website at: www.sqa.org.uk. There you will find the detailed content of special topic 'The Treaty of Union 1689–1740'.

The first section you will see is called 'Background'. The last section is called 'Perspective'. Neither of those sections will have any questions asked about them. They are **NOT** examined. That leaves four other sections, called issues, and each one of those issues has a question linked to it.

What do I have to do?

You will have five sources to use and four questions to answer. You will have 1 hour and 25 minutes to do that. That means you will have about 20 minutes to deal with each question so answers must be well structured and well developed. Put simply, that means you must do three things in each question:

1. You must do what you are asked to do.
2. You must refer to information in the source.
3. You must also include your own relevant recalled knowledge.

Each question also has its own particular process you must use to answer the question successfully. Later in this section there are sample answers to show you how to deal with the different questions.

What types of questions will I be asked?

There are FOUR different types of question. Each type will be in your exam paper.

Important: In this book the questions are listed as Type 1, 2, 3 and 4. This does **NOT** mean the questions will appear in that order in the exam. The different types of question can appear in **ANY** order.

> **Question Type 1 is a Source Evaluation Question worth 5 Marks.**

It will usually be identified with a question asking 'How useful is Source A as evidence…?'

In this type of question you are being asked to **judge** how good the source is as a piece of **historical evidence**:

- You will get up to a maximum of **2 marks** for writing about the source's origin (who wrote it or where the source first appeared) and its purpose (why the source was produced).

- You will only get up to **1 mark** by identifying and commenting briefly on where the source is from and why it was produced.

- For **2 marks** you will be expected to explain why its origin and purpose is important in the context of the question.

You will get up to a maximum of **2 marks** for **explaining why** the parts of the source you have selected are **useful** in terms of the question:

- There are no marks for just copying chunks of the source.

- Just listing relevant points from the source will only gain **1 mark**.

- For **2 marks** you must mention a point from the source and ALSO explain why the evidence you have selected is relevant to the question.

- Watch out for how that works in the examples that follow.

You will get up to a maximum of **2 marks** for using your own **detailed knowledge** as long as it is relevant to the question. This is called using relevant recall:

- You might, for example, want to consider if the source is entirely useful. A source will seldom be entirely valuable or useful. It will have limitations and it is up to you to explain what are these limits to usefulness.

- In this case a useful word to use is '**partly**'!

- You can give evidence to show that the source has its uses but also include information to suggest the source does not give the whole picture.

This looks like the total number of marks available for the question comes to 6, but there is only a possible total of 5 marks for this question. Stop to think how this helps you. If you had a weak section on origin and purpose you might only get 1 mark out of 2. But if your other two sections are well done, gaining the maximum of 2 marks per part, then you can still achieve the maximum total of 5 marks.

> **Question Type 2 is a Comparison Question worth 5 Marks.**

You will be asked to compare two points of view overall and in detail. It might **NOT** use the word 'compare' in the question.

The wording of the question will be something like 'To what extent does Source B agree with Source C about...?'

You will get up to a maximum of **2 marks** for an **overall comparison**. That means you should outline the main ideas or opinions or points of view in the two sources.

You will get up to a maximum of **4 marks** by **developing** your comparison in **detail**.

To get all 4 marks it is *not enough* just to list points of difference between the sources. In fact you might get **NO MARKS** for simply stating 'Source B says... but Source C says...'

- You MUST show that you understand the points made in the sources and explain in what ways they differ from each other or support each other.

- When you are explaining the differences or similarities it would be a good idea to use your own detailed knowledge to support your answer.

- There will always be **4** points of comparison for you to find in the sources.

- You will get **NO MARKS** for 'ghost' comparisons. In other words, no marks for writing 'Source B says... but Source C makes no mention of this.'

> Question Type 3 is a 'How far...' Question and is worth 10 Marks.

This question is to test your knowledge on one specific part of an issue, called a sub-issue. You can find all the sub-issues in the column called 'detailed descriptors' on the SQA syllabus website. The web address is given earlier in this chapter.

A question that asks 'How far does Source B explain the reasons for Scotland's economic difficulties before 1705?' tests your knowledge of the reasons for Scotland's economic problems.

To answer this question you must show you have **understood the reasons** for Scotland's economic problems that are included in the source and be able to explain those reasons. You can get up to **4 marks** just by doing that.

You must also include as much **accurate and relevant information** from your **own knowledge** about why Scotland had economic problems. You can get up to **7 marks** for this part of your answer.

As you write, ask yourself if the information you are including helps to reach a balanced answer – or are you just including stuff you know without really thinking about whether it answers the question?

What is Recall?

Recall means what you know about a certain topic. When evaluating a source, recall can mean using your knowledge to explain more fully a point already made in the source. It does not always have to be a completely new point.

> Question Type 4 is a 'How fully...' Question and is worth 10 Marks.

This question is to test your knowledge of a whole issue. Remember there are four issues in the syllabus that can be examined.

It could ask 'How fully does Source D illustrate the effects of the Treaty of Union on Scotland to 1740?'

The words 'effects of the Union to 1740' come straight from the issue title in the syllabus. Just as in the other 10 mark question, you can get up to **4 marks** for **explaining** the points in the source **relevant to the question**. You can then get up to **7 marks** for relevant **detailed recall** that helps answer the question directly.

Now do some training!

Read this before you start answering questions. It will help you to improve your answers.

Activities

1. After each worked example you will see another question for you to try yourself. Read again the advice about writing a good answer.

2. Write your answer.

3. Exchange your answer with a partner. Use the information you have about how marks are given to judge the value of your partner's answer. Return the marked answer. If there is any disagreement or difficulty ask your teacher to referee!

4. Once you have agreed the final mark take time to think about why you got the mark you did. Make two columns. Title one column 'What I did well'. Title the other column 'What I could improve on'. Use the feedback from your partner, your teacher and your own thoughts about your mark to complete the columns. Next time you do this type of question remember these columns!

The reason for doing this exercise is to understand and use the mark scheme. Once you know how marks are given you can structure your own answers to provide what markers are looking for.

Question Type 1 – Source Evaluation

Here is an example of a source evaluation question.

Source A describes the fate of a leading Covenanter, David Hackston, in July 1680. It is taken from the official decision of the Scottish Government office called the Privy Council.

Source A

'… his body be drawn backward on a hurdle to the cross of Edinburgh; that there be a high scaffold erected a little above the cross, where, in the first place, his right hand is to be struck off, and, after some time, his left hand; then he is to hanged up, and cut down alive, his bowels to be taken out and his heart shown to the people by the hangman; then his heart and bowels to be burned in a fire prepared for the purpose on the scaffold; that afterwards his head to be cut off, and his body divided into four quarters, with both his hands, to be affixed at St. Andrews; another quarter at Glasgow, a third at Leith, a fourth at Burntisland… that he be allowed to pray to God Almighty, but not to speak to the people…'

> **How useful is Source A as evidence of the treatment of Presbyterians in the 1680s?**
> **(5 marks)**

Here is a weak answer:

The source is useful because it gives a description of a Covenanter being executed. It says Hackston's 'right hand is to be struck off' and then his left hand. It describes how his bowels and heart would be taken out and burned and 'his body divided into four quarters, with both his hands, to be affixed at St. Andrews; another quarter at Glasgow, a third at Leith, a fourth at Burntisland'. The source is useful because it shows that Presbyterians were treated cruelly.

Why is this a weak answer?

This answer is weak mainly because:

(1) The answer fails to evaluate by referring to the origins and possible purpose of the source.

(2) The answer just describes the source.

(3) The answer is useful in the detail it gives about what happened to David Hackston, but mainly it just copies chunks of the source.

(4) The answer contains no recalled knowledge.

(5) There is no attempt to provide a balanced answer suggesting the source might have its limits as a useful piece of evidence.

Marks:

- There is no attempt to deal with origin or purpose (0 marks).

- It selects some relevant information from the source. However, it just lists some relevant points from the source. It does not explain why the evidence selected is relevant to the question (1 mark).

- There is no recall (0 marks).

Total achieved: 1 mark out of 5.

Here is a much better answer:

This source is partly useful for finding out about the experience of Presbyterians in the 1680s, but it has limits.

The source is from the Scottish Government in the 1680s. It shows you their attitude towards Covenanters who were extreme Presbyterians. The purpose is to send out a warning that extreme Presbyterians would not be tolerated. This makes the source very useful as primary evidence giving first hand detail about how brutally the Government acted.

The detail matches with my own knowledge. Presbyterians were harshly treated. The source describes how a leading Covenanter was publicly hung, drawn and quartered. The display of his body parts in different parts of Scotland was to serve as a warning to others. Some Presbyterians were tortured with thumbscrews and imprisoned with harsh conditions on the Bass Rock in the Firth of Forth.

The source does, however, have limits. It gives no information about how many Presbyterians fled to Holland in the 1680s to escape persecution. Viscount Claverhouse was nicknamed 'Bluidy Clavers' for his brutal treatment of the Covenaters in the 1680s. This period was also known as 'the Killing Time'.

Overall the source is quite useful for giving an impression but it tells us about one Covenanter's fate. We would need more evidence about the treatment of other Covenanters to form a fuller picture.

Why is this a much better answer?

It is a better answer because:

(1) It not only identifies the origin and purpose of the source but explains why each makes it a useful source (2 marks).

(2) It provides detail about the treatment of David Hackston and confirms his brutal treatment was not isolated. The candidate uses other recalled knowledge to confirm the brutal actions of the government in the 1680s. This makes it clear that the evidence selected is relevant to the question (2 marks).

(3) The answer provides a balanced evaluation of the usefulness of the source and includes more recall that helps evaluate the evidence in terms of the question asked (2 marks).

Marks

This answer scores highly simply by following the three stage marking scheme process. The maximum number of marks for a Type 1 question is 5 so even if this answer dropped a mark on a section, the writer would still gain full marks.

> Now try it yourself

Source B is from a letter written by Viscount Claverhouse to the Marquis of Queensberry on 3 May 1685.

Source B

'May it please your Grace. On Friday last, among the hills between Douglas and the Pentlands, we pursued two fellows a great way through the mosses, and in end seized them. They had no arms [weapons] about them, and denied they had any, but being asked if they would take the abjuration [oath of allegiance to Charles II required by the Test Act of 1681], the eldest of the two, called John Brown, refused it; nor would he swear not to rise in arms against the King, but said he knew no king; upon which, and there being found bullets and match in his house, and treasonable papers, I [had] cause [to] shoot him dead, which he suffered very unconcernedly...'

How useful is Source B as evidence of the treatment of Presbyterians in the 1680s?
(5 marks)

You should refer to:

- *the origin and possible purpose of the source*
- *the content of the source*
- *recalled knowledge.*

> Question Type 2 – The Comparison Question

Source C is from George Lockhart of Carnwath's Memoirs (1707).

Source C

'Whoever will impartially reflect upon this grand affair when this pretended payment of arrears [£20,000] was made, the place from whence the money came [London], the clandestine [secret] manner of obtaining and disposing of it, and lastly, that all the persons [excepting the Duke of Atholl] on whom it was bestowed, did vote for and promote the Union. Whoever, I say, will impartially reflect upon these particulars, must conclude, that the money was designed and bestowed [given out] for bribing members of Parliament.'

Source D is from the modern historian Professor C.A. Whatley.

> ### Source D
>
> 'No doubt many, probably most, men entered Parliament with hopes of some kind of preferment and personal pecuniary [monetary] advantage. While political management, including promises of posts and pensions and promotions, helped to secure pro-Union votes, such inducements, including cash bribes, persuaded only a handful of men to change sides. Lockhart's list of beneficiaries of Queen Anne's largesse [£20,000 payment] even includes men who were not members of Parliament and, in fact, most of the payments were of salary arrears. The longer a man had been in the Scottish Parliament, the more likely it was that he would vote for incorporation. Almost half of the commissioners in the Union Parliament had been elected or entered Parliament prior to the end of 1702; of these, nearly two-thirds voted in favour of most of the Articles of Union.'

> **How far does Source C agree with Source D about the role of bribery in getting the Treaty of Union passed by the Scottish Parliament?**
>
> *Compare the content overall and in detail.*
> **(5 marks)**

Here is a weak answer:

The two sources are about bribery during the Union debate. One thinks that bribery was used and the other doesn't. One says that £20,000 was 'designed and bestowed for bribing members of Parliament' and the other one says 'most, men entered Parliament with hopes of some kind of preferment and personal pecuniary advantage'. The sources are both about bribery, but they say different things.

Why is this a weak answer?

This is a weak answer because:

(1) There is no attempt to introduce the answer with an overall comparison.

(2) The writer does not identify what sources are being used at any time.

(3) The writer simply writes extracts from the sources and does not explain the point or meaning.

(4) The two extracts written from the sources are not about the same things so a direct comparison cannot be made.

Marks

There are only two points which *might* be considered as comparisons. At most this answer would get 2 marks out of 5.

Here is a much better answer:

Overall the sources are about the use of bribery during the Union debate in Scotland. Source C believes that the £20,000 was used as bribery to make Scottish politicians vote for Union whereas Source D claims that the use of rewards was not nearly as important because voting behaviour for the vast majority did not change. Lockhart was a Jacobite and hated the Union. Whatley is a modern historian who has undertaken the latest research in trying to reach a balanced conclusion.

In detail, Source C claims that the £20,000 pretended to be a payment of arrears, but was really a bribe whereas Source D disagrees because this money was genuinely paid out for arrears of salary in most cases. Source D also points out that some of those who were paid were not even in the Scottish Parliament to vote. This puts a question mark over how the payments from the £20,000 could be bribery.

Source C places great emphasis upon the £20,000 being secretly brought from London and distributed. Source D makes no mention of this point because it is not considered important. Source D is more concerned to prove that only a very few individuals changed their voting because of having received a money reward of some kind. Whatley could be referring to Lord Elibank as one individual who changed sides.

Source C argues that everyone who received money from the £20,000 voted for the Union except the Duke of Atholl. Source D believes that this is nonsense because those who were going to vote for the Union were going to do so anyway, but they still expected to be given posts, pensions and promotions.

Finally, Source D is the only one to point out that other factors influenced the way that individuals voted on the Union. Whatley believes that the length of time spent in the Scottish Parliament created an increased likelihood of voting for the Union.

It is hardly surprising that Sources C and D completely disagree about the role of bribery because one is written by a Jacobite and the other by a modern historian.

Why is this a much better answer?

It is a better answer because:

(1) The answer starts with an overall assessment which gains 1 mark. A second mark would also be given for identifying Lockhart as a biased Jacobite and Whatley as a more balanced modern historian.

(2) The answer then gives at least four direct comparisons.

(3) The comparisons are relevant and connected to each other.

(4) The comparisons are identified by the author's name.

(5) Recall is used to explain attitudes or details mentioned in the extracts. The recall example given is about Lord Elibank.

(6) The answer contains comparisons of opinion but provides reasons for the differences.

Marks

This answer gains 5 marks out of 5. This answer scored highly simply by following the marking scheme process.

> **Now try it yourself**

Source E is from the modern historian W. Ferguson.

Source E

'The Equivalent, indeed, had a major part to play in predisposing [getting members] to favour the treaty…
It must also be borne in mind that the sums involved [from the £20,000] were in sterling. To assess their real value in Scotland in 1706–7 is extremely difficult, but a start can be made by multiplying by twelve to get the reckoning in Scots money. In many cases, too, the sum would have to be doubled because of later disbursements [money given] from the Equivalent. No Scottish laird [landowner] of the time would have regarded such a sum as a mere trifle [small amount]…

 … the Squadrone was gulled [tricked] into the Court's interest by a tacit promise [an unwritten understanding], later broken, that as nominees of the directors of the Company of Scotland, they would be allowed to handle that part of the Equivalent intended to recoup [reimburse] the shareholders.'

Source F is from the modern historian Professor C.A. Whatley.

Source F

'The significance of compensation [Equivalent] for Company of Scotland subscribers in easing the passage of the Union should not be overestimated, however, even with the Squadrone. Roxburghe [leader of the Squadrone], for instance, had no direct interest in the company. Among members of parliament generally, more non-stockholders voted in favour than did those who held company stock.'

To what extent does Source E agree with Source F about the role of bribery in deciding the union?
Compare the content overall and in detail.
(5 marks)

Question Type 3 – the 'How far...' Question

This is the question that asks about a specific part of an issue and wants to find out how much you know on the subject. A useful way to start an answer to this type of question is to say '**partly**'. That gives a basic answer to the question, 'How far…'

The source will provide relevant information but will not give the whole picture. That allows you to include other information relevant to the answer from your own knowledge in order to provide a full answer.

There are two phases to any answer to this type of question:

(1) You must select relevant points from the source and develop each point with recalled detailed knowledge. There are **4 marks** available for doing this.

(2) You must then bring in your own knowledge to show there are other points relevant to the answer that are not in the sources. This part is worth up to **7 marks**.

Here is an example of a 'how far' question:

Source G is from the Earl of Mar's Declaration at Braemar on 9 September 1715.

> ### Source G
>
> 'Now is the time for all good men to show their zeal for His Majesty's [James VIII] service, whose cause is so deeply concerned, and the relief of our native country from oppression, and a foreign yoke too heavy for us and our posterity to bear; and to endeavour the restoring, not only of our rightful and native king, but also our country to its ancient, free, and independent constitution under him whose ancestors have reigned over us for so many generations.'

> **How far does Source G explain the reasons for supporting the Jacobite rebellion in 1715?**
>
> *Use the source and recalled knowledge.*
> **(10 marks)**

Here is a weak answer:

The source gives quite good evidence of reasons for supporting the Jacobites. It says that 'all good men to show their zeal for His Majesty's service'. This shows they wanted to make James king.

The source says that supporting the Jacobites would relieve 'our native country from oppression'. This means that Scotland wasn't doing well after 1707.

It says that Scotland was under a heavy 'foreign yoke' after 1707. This means the rule of England.

The source argues that by putting a Stuart king back on the throne, Scotland would get its 'its ancient, free, and independent constitution'.

Why is this a weak answer?

This answer is weak mainly because:

(1) The answer relies almost entirely on the information provided in the source.

(2) There is very little detailed recalled knowledge used to develop the points.

(3) There is no mention of any other reasons for supporting the Jacobites that is necessary in this sort of evaluation question. In other words, the candidate ignores the 'How far' part of the question.

Marks

The candidate only uses the source and makes the most limited development points so will only gain at most 2 out of the available 4 marks for this part. There is no recall in terms of the question to provide any balance, so this candidate gets 0 out of 7 marks available for this part. Total achieved: 2 marks out of 10.

Here is a much better answer:

The source partly gives good evidence about why there was support for the Jacobites in 1715. The Earl of Mar was the leader of the 1715 rebellion. His declaration is trying to attract supporters by saying 'all good men to show their zeal for His Majesty's service'. This was the traditional appeal of Jacobitism, the chance to put a Stuart king back on to the throne. It appealed in particular to the Highland clans.

The source mentions that the Jacobite rebellion would save Scotland from oppression. Mar was quick to say that the British Government was planning to impose more taxes upon Scotland. These would even include cocks and hens in addition to land, malt, cattle and sheep.

The source argues that Scotland is oppressed and can only prosper if the Jacobites can win back Scotland's independence. The motto on the Jacobite flag was 'No Hanoverian!', 'No Popery!', 'No Union!' This shows how the Jacobites tried to make the broadest possible appeal. They were anti-Catholic, but wanted to restore a Catholic monarch to the throne and end the Union of 1707.

The Union was not popular right from the start. This explains why Article 22 had an ammendment making sure that the new British MPs would be elected by the members of the last Scottish Parliament. This aimed to prevent

Jacobites being elected. A number of modern historians agree that the size of support given to the Jacobites in 1715 can only be explained by allowing for the unpopularity of the Union. Professor Whatley and D.Szechi agree about this. The size of the Jacobite army in 1689 was about 5000 men, but in 1715 it rose to about 10,000. About 12% of the total Scottish male population served on the Jacobite side during the rebellion. This was more men than in any other Jacobite rebellion, including 1745. The support from the Highland clans was more widespread in 1715 compared to 1689.

Being forced out by the chief to fight for the Jacobites doesn't make sense as an explanation of why so many supported the Jacobites. Mar and others did force some tenants and clansmen to come out and fight, but this was partly because the rebellion took place in harvest time when men did important jobs. There were other clansmen who came out to fight against the wishes of their chief. These included the Grants of Glenmoriston and Glenurquhart and the Atholl men.

The idea that many clans supported the Jacobites because of an anti-Campbell hostility doesn't stand up as an explanation. The Campbells of Glenorchy fought for the Jacobites and 16 clans who might have good cause to hate the Campbell House of Argyll didn't always support the Jacobites.

Jacobite support did have a religious element to it. In 1715 no Presbyterian clan supported the Jacobites. Jacobite support among the Highland clans came from 15 Episcopalian, six Catholic and five mixed-denomination clans.

Episcopalian landowners in the north-east of Scotland supported the Jacobites in large numbers. This was unlike in 1689. This was partly because there was a Presbyterian settlement of the Church in Scotland in 1690 and the Union of 1707 confirmed this, but the effects of Union after 1707 must also be allowed for. These landowners had also convinced themselves that the time was right for a Jacobite rebellion. Many of them knew each other and a number of unusual events, including an eclipse, seemed to be a sign from God that a rebellion would be a success. The Jacobites were also convinced that they would receive French and English help.

The failure of the 1707 Union to deliver immediate economic prosperity seems to have had a considerable effect upon supporting the Jacobites. Widespread smuggling after 1707 is another indicator of the Union's unpopularity. Source G gives a general idea that the Union was unpopular but doesn't give specific reasons to explain support for the Jacobites in 1715.

Why is this a much better answer?

It is a better answer because:

(1) It selects information from the source and uses recalled knowledge to develop each point made.

(2) It provides a balance to the answer by using a lot of recall about factors influencing support for the Jacobites.

(3) It ends with a short conclusion that shows the candidate has understood the question and thought about its meaning.

Marks

This answer scores highly simply by following the marking scheme process. The candidate uses the source and develops the points well so gains 4 out of 4 marks.

There is a lot of recall and most of it is relevant. However, the answer would have benefited from being able to include specific grievances about the effects of Union. You will be able to make this answer perfect after re-reading pages 90–92. The answer as it is would gain 9 out of 10 marks.

> **Now try it yourself**

Source H is from a letter written by the Earl of Mar in 1711.

Source H

'The English, as most of the Scots are, seem to be weary of the Union, but when they first came to think of it seriously, I doubt of their quitting it. What seems to be the opinion or resolution of our countrymen here for relieving us of this hardship is either to dissolve the Union or else an Act of Parliament reversing what is done by the House of Lords and putting us in the same place and condition as we were before... As to dissolving the Union in a Parliamentary way, I despair of it, or if it were possible in doing it, they would fix the succession, and in that case Scotland would lose any awe it could have over England... I believe never were people [the Scots] in harder circumstances... If we saw the possibility of getting free of Union without a civil war, we would have some comfort but that I'm afraid is impossible.'

> **How far does Source H show the reasons why so many Scots supported the Jacobites in 1715?**
> **(10 marks)**

Question Type 4 – The 'How fully...' Question

This is the question that asks about a specific issue within the syllabus and wants to find out how much you know on the subject. A useful way to start an answer to this type of question is to say '**partly**'. That gives a basic answer to the question, 'How fully...'

The source will provide relevant information but will not give the whole picture. That allows you to include other information relevant to the answer from your own knowledge in order to provide a full answer.

There are two phases to any answer to this type of question:

(1) You must select relevant points from the source and develop each point with recalled detailed knowledge. There are **4 marks** available for doing this.

(2) You must then bring in your own knowledge to show there are other points relevant to the answer that are not in the sources. This part is worth up to **7 marks**.

Here is an example of a 'How fully...' question:

Source I is from the House of Lords Journal, June 1713.

> **Source I**
>
> 'The Question is put to the House:
> That permission be given to bring in a Bill, to end the Union; and for restoring each Kingdom to their Rights and Privileges as they had been at the time when the Union was first passed…
> That charging Scotland with this Malt Tax, will be a violation of the 14th article of the Treaty of Union; by which it was clearly stated 'that Scotland shall not be charged with any Malt Tax during this war'.
> We must regard it as unjust, to make that part of the United Kingdom pay any part of this tax.'

> How fully does Source I explain the effects of the Treaty of Union on Scotland after 1707?
> (10 marks)

Here is a weak answer to the question:

Source I records the introduction of a bill to the House of Lords in 1713 to repeal the 1707 Treaty of Union. The main reason for this is given as the introduction of the Malt Tax in 1713. This is argued as breaking Article 14 of the Treaty of Union, which agreed that there would be no increase in the amount of tax on malt for the duration of the War of the Spanish Succession 1701–1714. The 1713 Malt Tax was viewed as being unjust as a result.

Why is this a weak answer?

This answer is weak mainly because:

(1) The candidate only really makes the point about the 1713 Malt Tax being a key moment in bringing about a move to dissolve the Union and how this broke Article 14 of Union. This can only get at most 2 marks out of 4.

(2) There is one point of recall mentioned about the Spanish War of Succession. This gives 1 mark out of a possible 7.

(3) The main weakness in this answer is that the candidate does not move away from the content of the sources. This answer would get no more than 3 out of 10 marks.

Here's how it could be a better answer (but not brilliant!):

Source I partly explains the effect of the Union. The Malt Tax 1713 was thought to have broken Article 14 of Union. This said that no additional tax would be placed upon malt in Scotland as long as the War of the Spanish Succession was still being fought. Taxes imposed upon linen and salt in 1711 were also very unpopular and thought to break the spirit of the terms of Union.

Union failed to deliver immediate economic prosperity. Some industries, including linen, struggled after 1707. Agriculture showed little improvement. Jacobite opposition to Union continued after 1707. There was a minor rising in 1708 and a major one in 1715. Presbyterians opposed various religious changes after 1707 as well.

Source I really only mentions the unpopularity of the Malt Tax in causing a vote to repeal the Union in 1713. There were many other reasons for the unpopularity of the Union by this time.

Why is this answer better but still not brilliant?

(1) This answer at least brings in relevant recall and shows an understanding of the importance of other factors in bringing about an attempt to dissolve the Union. This answer would still only gain 3 out of 4 for developing the source but could gain 3 out of 7 marks for relevant recall, gaining a total of 6 out of 10 marks.

(2) The answer needs to consider the impact of Union upon specific industries, in different parts of Scotland, by giving examples. Why did the Scottish linen industry struggle? This could have led to mention of a lack of funding available for investment in Scottish industry. There was a need to consider the widespread growth of smuggling because of increased customs duties. This could have included mention of smuggling tobacco from the American colonies. Examples of riots and the treatment of excisemen could have been given.

(3) The specific effects of the Union upon both the Highlands and Lowlands need to be explained. Widespread disappointment with the Union could have been related to the size of support for the Jacobites in the 1715 rebellion. The angry reaction of Presbyterians to various religious changes after 1707 also need to be considered, along with other reasons for the Scottish political elite being disappointed with Union by 1713.

(4) The whole course cannot be covered in this answer but equally it must be understood that this question needs an overview of the main points in the course to be successful. In this sense, the summary table on page 104 is very useful. It allows you to use several points for recall and show that, in theory, the Union of 1707 addressed Scottish concerns, but in reality problems remained after 1707. You could use this as a final concluding section to your answer.

Advice to improve:

To improve this answer the candidate would just have to provide more detailed recall giving a wider review of the effects of the union.

Now try it yourself

Source J is from I.D. Whyte's *An Historical Geography of Scotland* (1983).

Source J

'Undoubtedly [Union] was not an immediate cure for Scotland's economic ills, and there were both gains and losses in the short term. The collapse of the woollen industry, which was in difficulties before 1707, was inevitable in the face of English competition. With the demise [disappearance] of fine woollens, linen became Scotland's premier manufacture. England provided a major market. The droving trade expanded after 1707 but not dramatically. Grain exports also increased, but it is uncertain how much of this was due merely to better weather conditions. Agricultural improvement did take place but very slowly. Such developments as occurred owed little to the Union, being continuation of trends which had existed before 1707.'

How fully does Source J explain the effects of the 1707 Union on Scotland by 1740?
(10 marks)

References

References for sources

For all photographs please see page ii.

Chapter 1

Source 1.1 adapted from W. Robson *Crown Parliament and People*, p54

Source 1.3 RPS, 1689/3/16. Date accessed: 12 July 2008. From the website The Scottish Parliament Project

Source 1.4 RPS, 1689/3/19. Date accessed: 12 July 2008. From the website The Scottish Parliament Project

Source 1.5 A.M. MacKenzie *Orain Iain Luim: Songs of John MacDonald Bard of Keppoch*, pp203–213

Source 1.6 A.I. Macinnes *Clanship Commerce and the House of Stuart*, p244; pp247–8

Source 1.7 B. Lenman *The Jacobite Risings in Britain 1689–1746*, p47

Source 1.9 The Earl of Balcarres *The Battle of Killiecrankie* (27 July 1689) from R. Goring *Scotland: The Autobiography*, pp93–94

Source 1.15 R. Goring *Scotland: The Autobiography*, p95

Source 1.16 D.J. MacDonald *Slaughter Under Trust*, pp83–84

Source 1.17 The National Archives of Scotland and Learning and Teaching Scotland 2004, p6

Source 1.18 R. Goring *Scotland: The Autobiography*, pp97–8

Source 1.30 SQA Higher History Paper 2 2007

Source 1.32 adapted from www.scottishexecutive.gov.uk/News/News-Extras/146

Source 1.33 D. Watt *The Price of Scotland: Darien, Union and the Wealth of Nations*, p149

Source 1.34 www.bbc.co.uk/history/british/civil_war_revolution/ scotland_darien_03.shtml

Source 1.35 D. Watt *The Price of Scotland: Darien, Union and the Wealth of Nations*, p6

Source 1.36 http://special.lib.gla.ac.uk/exhibns/month/may2005.html

Source 1.38 P.H. Scott *1707: The Union of Scotland and England*, p17

Source 1.39 W. Ferguson *Scotland 1689 to the Present: The Edinburgh History of Scotland*, Vol. 4, pp78–79

Source 1.40 *Ane End of Ane Auld Sang: Scotland and the Treaty of Union 1690s–1715*, p14

Source 1.41 Scotland's Story Vol. 22, p22

Source 1.43 SQA Higher History Paper 2 2004

Source 1.44 SQA Higher History Paper 2 2001

Source 1.45 Hutchesons Grammar School Source Booklet, Acts of the Parliament of Scotland, .P.S xi, 107, c.6

Source 1.47 www.parliament.uk/actofunion/03_04_quieter.html

Source 1.49 T.M. Devine *Scotland's Empire 1600–1815*, p52

Source 1.53 *1701 The Act of Union* DVD

Chapter 2

Source 2.2 SQA Higher History Paper 2 Exam 2002

Source 2.3 SQA Higher History Paper 2 Exam 1999

Source 2.4 A.I. Macinnes *Union and Empire: The Making of the United Kingdom in 1707*, p133; p231

Source 2.5 SQA Higher History Paper 2 2007

Source 2.7 SQA Higher History Paper 2 1999

Source 2.9 P.H. Scott *1707 The Union of Scotland and England*, p56

Source 2.11 P.H. Scott *1707 The Union of Scotland and England*, p55

Source 2.12 P.H. Scott *1707 The Union of Scotland and England*, p25; p31

Source 2.13 SQA Paper 2 1994 and SQA Paper 2 1996

Source 2.16 The Act of Union 1707 DVD

Source 2.17 SQA Higher History Paper 2 2000

Source 2.18 Taken from a booklet compilation from Hutchesons Grammar School Glasgow

Source 2.20 T. Devine *Scotland's Empire 1600–1815*, p63

Source 2.21 Taken from a booklet compilation from Hutchesons Grammar School Glasgow

Source 2.22 P.H. Scott *1707 The Union of Scotland and England*, p29

Source 2.23 P.H. Scott *1707 The Union of Scotland and England*, p33

Source 2.24 P.H. Scott *1707 The Union of Scotland and England*, p59

Source 2.25 P.H. Scott *1707 The Union of Scotland and England*, p50

Source 2.26 C. Whatley *The Scots and the Union*, p55

Source 2.27 A.I. Macinnes *Union and Empire: The Making of the United Kingdom in 1707*, p27

Source 2.29 C. Whatley *The Scots and the Union*, p33

Chapter 3

Source 3.1 SQA Higher History Paper 2 2004

Source 3.2 D. Thomson *An Introduction to Gaelic Poetry*, p127

Source 3.3 *The Complete Illustrated Poems, Songs and Ballads of Robert Burns*, p410

Source 3.4 SQA Higher History Paper 2 2005

Source 3.5 A.I. Macinnes *Union and Empire: The Making of the United Kingdom in 1707*, p294

Source 3.6 T.M. Devine (ed.) *Scotland and the Union 1707–2007*, p67

Source 3.7 SQA Higher History Paper 2 2005

Source 3.8 William Ferguson *Scotland's Relations with England: A Survey to 1707*, p249

Source 3.9 SQA Higher History Paper 2 1998

Source 3.10 P.H. Scott *1707 The Union of Scotland and England*, p40

Source 3.11 P.H. Scott *1707 The Union of Scotland and England*, p42

Source 3.12 P.H. Scott *1707 The Union of Scotland and England*, p57

Source 3.13 D. Daiches *Scotland and the Union*, p137

Source 3.14 P.H. Scott *1707 The Union of Scotland and England*, p40

Chapter 4

Source 4.2 www.telusplanet.net/public/prescotj/data/music/camyeoer.html

Source 4.3 D. Szechi *1715 The Great Jacobite Rebellion*, p15

Source 4.4 A.I. Macinnes *Clanship, Commerce and the House of Stuart 1603–1788*, p163

Source 4.5 A.I. Macinnes *Clanship, Commerce and the House of Stuart 1603–1788*, p245

Source 4.6 K.M. Brown *Kingdom or Province? Scotland and the Regal Union*, p192

Source 4.7 A.I. Macinnes *Clanship, Commerce and the House of Stuart 1603–1788*, p180

Source 4.8 D. Love *Jacobite Stories*, p24

Source 4.9 D. Szechi *1715 The Great Jacobite Rebellion*, p63

Source 4.10 B. Lenman *The Jacobite Risings in Britain 1689–1746*, pp126–7

Source 4.12 SQA Higher History Paper 2 1996

Source 4.13 A.I. Macinnes *Clanship, Commerce and the House of Stuart 1603–1788*, pp191–2

Source 4.14 Mairead McKerracher *The Jacobite Dictionary*, p204

Source 4.16 D. Szechi *George Lockhart of Carnwath 1689–1727: A Study in Jacobitism*, p115

Source 4.19 M. Lynch *Scotland A New History*, p323

Source 4.22 R. Goring *Scotland: The Autobiography*, pp121–124

Source 4.23 R. Goring *Scotland: The Autobiography*, pp118–120

Source 4.24 A.I. Macinnes *Clanship, Commerce and the House of Stuart 1603–1788*, p193

Source 4.25 M. Lynch *Scotland A New History*, p325

Source 4.32 A. Simmons *Burt's Letters from the North of Scotland*, pp50–51

Source 4.33 M. Magnusson *Scotland: The Story of a Nation*, p553

Source 4.35 M. Lynch *Scotland A New History*, p345

Chapter 5

Source 5.1 www.bbchistorymagazine.com/union.asp

Source 5.2 N. Ferguson *The War of the World: History's Age of Hatred*, plxiii

Source 5.3 C. Whatley *The Scots and the Union*, p53

Source 5.4 K.M. Brown *Kingdom or Province: Scotland and the Regal Union, 1603–1715*, p188

Source 5.5 J. Paxman *The English: A Portrait of a People*, pp43–4

Source 5.6 Sunday Herald 4 November 2007

Source 5.7 A.I. Macinnes *Clanship, Commerce and the House of Stuart 1603–1788*, p193

Source 5.8 A.I. Macinnes *Union and Empire: The Making of the United Kingdom in 1707*, p325

Source 5.9 www.bbchistorymagazine.com/union

Source 5.10 A.I. Macinnes *Clanship, Commerce and the House of Stuart 1603–1788*, p193

Source 5.12 www.bbc.co.uk/iplayer/episode/b00jzm7c/Question_Time_23_04_2009/

Source 5.13 P.H. Scott quoting C.J. Watson *Still in bed with an elephant*, p104

Preparing for Paper 2

A D. Love Scottish *Covenanting Stories: Tales from the Killing Time*, p86

B D. Love *Covenanting Stories: Tales from the Killing Time*, p180

C SQA Higher History Paper 2 1991

D T.M. Devine (ed.) *Scotland and the Union 1707–2007*, p30

E W. Ferguson *Scotland's Relations with England: A Survey to 1707*, p249

F T.M. Devine (ed.) *Scotland and the Union 1707–2007*, p34

G www.jacobite.ca/documents/17150909.htm

H SQA Higher History Paper 2 1996

I SQA Higher History Paper 2 2008

J SQA Higher History Paper 2 1994

Bibliography

Brown, K. M. (1993) *Kingdom or Province: Scotland and the Regal Union, 1603–1715*, MacMillan Press Ltd

Burns, R. (1990) from *The Complete Illustrated Poems, Songs and Ballads of Robert Burns*, Chancellor Press

Daiches, D. (1977) *Scotland and the Union*, Book Club Associates

Dargie, R. (1999) *Scotland and the Union 1690–1715*, HarperCollins

Davidson, N. (2003) *Discovering the Scottish Revolution 1692–1746*, Pluto Press

Deary, T. (2005) *Horrible Histories: Edinburgh*, Scholastic

Deary, T. (1998) *Horrible Histories: Bloody Scotland*, Scholastic 1998

Devine, T.M. (2000) *The Scottish Nation 1700–2000*, Penguin

Devine, T.M. (2004) *Scotland's Empire 1600–1815*, Penguin

Devine, T.M. (2008) *Scotland and the Union 1707–2007*, Edinburgh University Press

Donaldson, G. and Morpeth, R.S. (1977) *A Dictionary of Scottish History*, John Donald Publishers

Ferguson, N. (2006) *The War of the World: History's Age of Hatred*, Allen Lane/Penguin Books

Ferguson, N. (1999) *The Pity of War*, Penguin

Ferguson, W. (1978) *Scotland 1689 to the Present: The Edinburgh History of Scotland*, Vol. 4, Oliver and Boyd

Ferguson, W. (1977) *Scotland's Relations with England: A Survey to 1707*, John Donald Publishers Ltd

Fry, M. (2006) *The Union: England, Scotland and the Treaty of 1707*, Birlinn Ltd

Goring, R. (2008) *Scotland: The Autobiography*, Penguin

Herman, A. (2006) *The Scottish Enlightenment: The Scots' Invention of the Modern World*, Harper Perennial

Herman, A. (2001) *How the Scots Invented the Modern World*, Three Rivers Press

Hunter, J. (1995) *A Dance Called America: Scottish Highlands, the USA and Canada*, Mainstream

Jamieson, B. (1998) *Ane End of Ane Auld Sang: Scotland and the Treaty of Union 1690s–1715*, Scottish Consultative Committee on the Curriculum

Keay, J. and Keay, J. (1994) *Collins Encyclopaedia of Scotland*, Harper Collins

Lenman, B. (1980) *The Jacobite Risings in Britain 1689–1746*, Eyre Methuen

Love, D. (2007) *Jacobite Stories*, Neil Wilson Publishing Limited

Love, D. (2005) *Scottish Covenanting Stories: Tales from the Killing Time*, Neil Wilson Publishing

Lynch, M. (2007) *Oxford Companion to Scottish History*, Oxford University Press

Lynch, M. (1992) *Scotland A New History*, Pimlico

MacDonald, D.J. (1982) *Glencoe 1692: Slaughter Under Trust 2nd Edition*, Delaware Free Press

Macinnes, A.I. (1996) *Clanship, Commerce and the House of Stuart*, Tuckwell Press Ltd

Bibliography

Macinnes, A.I. (207) *Union and Empire: The Making of the United Kingdom in 1707*, Cambridge University Press

MacKenzie, A.M. (1973) *Orain Iain Luim: Songs of John MacDonald Bard of Keppoch* The Scottish Academic Press for the Scottish Gaelic Texts Society (Edinburgh)

MacLeod, J. (1996) *Highlanders: A History of the Gaels*, Hodder and Stoughton

McLynn, F. (1985) *The Jacobites*, Routledge and Kegan Paul

McKerracher, M. (2007) *The Jacobite Dictionary*, Neil Wilson Publishing

Magnusson, M. (2001) *Scotland: The Story of a Nation*, HarperCollins

Mitchison, R. (1977) *A History of Scotland*, Methuen and Co. Ltd

Patrick, D.J. and Whatley, C.A. (2007) *Persistence, Principle and Patriotism in the Making of the Union of 1707: The Revolution, Scottish Parliament and the Squadrone Volante*, The Historical Association and Blackwell Publishing

Paxman, J. (1999) *The English: A Portrait of a People*, Penguin

RCAHMS, NAS and Historic Scotland (2007) *The Act of Union 1707* DVD

Robinson, T. (1999) *Kings and Queens*, Random House Children's Books

Robson, W. (2002) *Crown Parliament and People*, Oxford University Press

Rogers, P. (2005) *Pope and the Destiny of the Stuarts: History, Politics, and Mythology in the Age of Queen Anne*, Edinburgh University Press

Rosie, G. (2005) *Curious Scotland: Tales from a Hidden History*, Granta Books

Scott, P.H. (2006) *The Union of 1707: Why and How*, The Saltire Society

Scott, P.H. (1998) *Still in Bed with an Elephant*, The Saltire Society

Scott, P.H. (1979) *1707 The Union of Scotland and England*, W and R Chambers Ltd

Simmons, A. (1998) *Burt's Letters from the North of Scotland*, Birlinn

Smout, T.C. (1977) *A History of the Scottish People 1560–1830*, Fontana

SQA Higher History Paper 2 (various years) and Higher History Arrangements Documents valid from 2010

Szechi, D. (2002) *George Lockhart of Carnwath 1689–1727: A Study in Jacobitism* Tuckwell Press Ltd

Szechi, D. (2006) *1715 The Great Jacobite Rebellion*, Yale University Press

Thomson, D. (1990) *An Introduction to Gaelic Poetry*, Edinburgh University Press

Watt, D. (2007) *The Price of Scotland: Darien, Union and the Wealth of Nations*, Luath Press Ltd

Whatley, C. (2006) *The Scots and the Union*, Edinburgh University Press

Wilson, A.J., Brogan, D. and McGrail, F. (1991) *Ghostly Tales and Sinister Stories of Old Edinburgh*, Mainstream Publishing

Winn, C. (2007) *I Never Knew that about Scotland*, Ebury Press

Websites

www.parliament.uk/actofunion/

news.scotsman.com/theunion/Darien-Venture-was-a-good.3280689.jp

www.bbc.co.uk/history/british/civil_war_revolution/scotland_darien_03.shtml

www.scottishexecutive.gov.uk/News/News-Extras/146

www.history.ac.uk/reviews/paper/glickman.html

www.rahbarnes.demon.co.uk/clai1689.htm

www.itraveluk.co.uk/content/659.html

www.battlefieldstrust.com/resource-centre/stuart-rebellions/ battleview.asp?BattleFieldId=70

www.telusplanet.net/public/prescotj/data/music/camyeoer.html

websiterepository.ed.ac.uk/news/scotlandunion/debating.html

www.historycentral.com/dates/1700ad.html

www.accessmylibrary.com/coms2/summary_0286-24646087_ITM

www.questia.com/PM.qst?a=o&docId=103049348

www.xs4all.nl/~monarchs/madmon.html

www.bbc.co.uk/iplayer/episode/b00jzm7c/Question_Time_23_04_2009/

www.youtube.com/watch?v=KdRSJJPXKIs

www.youtube.com/watch?v=QDsmU6v2Egg

www.youtube.com/watch?v=rubzQiWrS5g

www.youtube.com/watch?v=4L_2tZ51C7A

Timeline

1680–88	Presbyterians persecuted by James VII (& II)
1688	10 June: James Francis Edward Stuart born (James VIII) 5 November: William of Orange arrived in England James VII fled to France
1689	14 March: Scottish Parliament opened 4 April: Scottish Parliament decided that James had forfeited the crown Scottish Parliament passes the Claim of Right and Articles of Grievance 11 May: William and Mary accept the Scottish Crown 27 July: Battle of Killiecrankie between Jacobites and Government armies 21 August: Jacobites retreat from Dunkeld
1690	1 May: Battle of Cromdale – the Jacobites are defeated 7 June: Presbyterian settlement of the Church in Scotland 12 July: James VII and the Jacobites defeated by William of Orange at the Battle of the Boyne in Ireland
1692	13 February: The Massacre of Glencoe The Treaty of Limerick: Ireland conquered by William
1688–97	Nine Years' War between England and France
1695	The Bank of Scotland founded The Company of Scotland founded A new law was implemented to establish English speaking schools in the Highlands in order to 'root out the Gaelic language'
1698	2 November: 1st expedition to Darien arrived
1699	May: Darien abandoned November: 2nd expedition to Darien arrived
1700	March: Darien settlers surrendered to the Spanish Charles II of Spain died.
1701	6 September: James VII (& II) died English Act of Settlement
1701–14	War of the Spanish Succession between England and France
1702	King William III (& II) died Negotiations for Union fail
1703	Scottish Act of Security Scottish Act Anent Peace and War The Scottish Wine Act

Timeline

1704	Scottish Wool Act August: Battle of Blenheim. This was a British army victory over the French
1705	5 February: Aliens Act 11 April: Crew of the Worcester hanged 1 September: The Duke of Hamilton allowed the Queen to nominate the Scottish Commissioners to negotiate Union 15 November: Aliens Act repealed
1706	16 April–11 July 1706: Scottish and English Commissioners met in London to negotiate the articles of union October 1706 – January 1707: Scottish Parliament approved the Articles of Union 12 November: Act for Securing the Protestant Religion and the Presbyterian Church Government passed by the Scottish Parliament
1707	January: the Treaty of Union approved by the Scottish Parliament 28 April 1707: Scottish Parliament dissolved 1 May 1707: the first British Parliament met
1708	Privy Council abolished
1709	English Law of Treason introduced into Scotland
1711	Taxes on linen and salt
1712	Toleration Act Patronage Act Yule Vacance Act
1713	Malt Tax The House of Lords voted narrowly not to dissolve the Union
1714	August George I becomes the first Hanoverian British monarch
1715	Louis XIV died Jacobite Rebellion
1719	Jacobite Rebellion
1725	Malt Tax Shawfield Riot
1736	Porteous Riot

Places in Scotland Mentioned in This Book

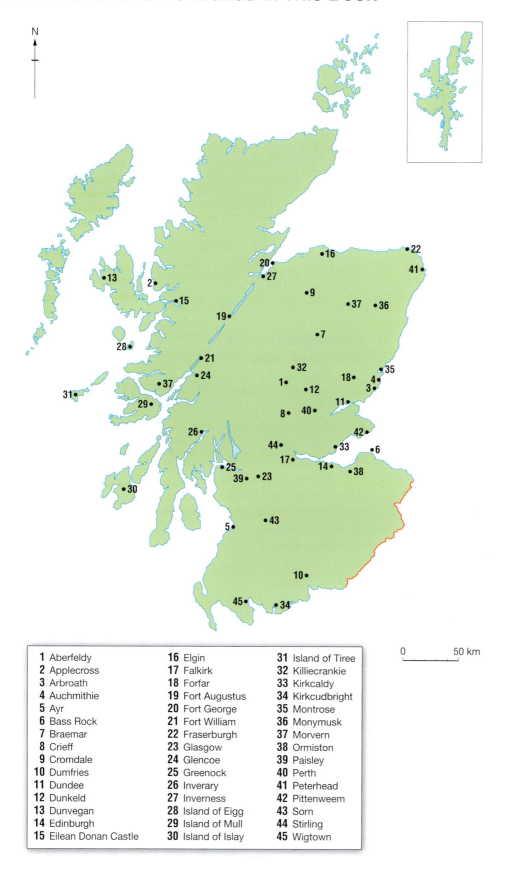

1 Aberfeldy	16 Elgin	31 Island of Tiree
2 Applecross	17 Falkirk	32 Killiecrankie
3 Arbroath	18 Forfar	33 Kirkcaldy
4 Auchmithie	19 Fort Augustus	34 Kirkcudbright
5 Ayr	20 Fort George	35 Montrose
6 Bass Rock	21 Fort William	36 Monymusk
7 Braemar	22 Fraserburgh	37 Morvern
8 Crieff	23 Glasgow	38 Ormiston
9 Cromdale	24 Glencoe	39 Paisley
10 Dumfries	25 Greenock	40 Perth
11 Dundee	26 Inverary	41 Peterhead
12 Dunkeld	27 Inverness	42 Pittenweem
13 Dunvegan	28 Island of Eigg	43 Sorn
14 Edinburgh	29 Island of Mull	44 Stirling
15 Eilean Donan Castle	30 Island of Islay	45 Wigtown

Index

absolutism, Catholic 3
Act Anent Peace and War 1703 34, 45, 108
Act for Securing the Protestant Religion and Presbyterian Church Government 1706 53, 74
Act of Security 1703 33, 34, 35, 36, 45, 108
agriculture 103, 109
Aikenhead, Thomas 15
Alien Act 1705 38, 45, 53, 66, 67
Anglophobia 43
Anne, Queen 4, 33, 34–7, 40, 42, 48, 57, 67, 68, 79, 106, 108
Argyll, John Campbell, 2nd Duke of 11, 43, 64, 67, 85, 87, 99, 102
Articles of Grievance 3, 108
Articles of Union 49, 50, 57–8, 67–73, 74–6, 95, 103, 109
amendments 49, 55, 69, 70, 72, 77

Bass Rock 17, 19
Belhaven, John Hamilton, 2nd Lord 47–8
Bible 15, 101
bishops 19, 47, 82
black cattle trade 31, 97–9, 102, 103
Black Watch Regiment 96
Blair, Tony 111
Blenheim, Battle of 1704 37, 54
Borland, Francis 28
Boyne, Battle of the 1690 9
Breadalbane, Earl of 11
bribery 60–6
British Parliament 69, 70, 74–5, 76, 80, 94–5
Brown, K.M. 82, 108
Brown, P.H. 106
burghs 44, 58, 72

Burns, Robert 61, 92
Burt, Edmund 100

Campbells 5, 6, 9–14, 58, 82, 85
Captain Green Affair 37
Carlos II, King of Spain 32
Carlyle, Alexander 93–4
Carstares, William 19
Carthagena 26, 27, 28
Catholicism 2–3, 15–19, 47, 53, 55, 65, 70, 82–3, 96
Charles I 15, 54
Charles II 15, 16, 18
Charnley, J. 108
Church of Scotland 53, 55, 74
civil war 41, 54
Claim of Right 1689 3, 108
Claverhouse, James Graham, Viscount 5, 7, 8, 16
Clerk of Penicuik, John 50–1, 54, 65, 67, 101–2
Cockburn of Ormiston, John 103
colonies 2, 20–9, 34, 41, 51–2, 55, 74, 102, 104, 108–9
Company of Scotland 25, 27, 29, 37, 63, 72, 75
constitutional monarchy 45
Cornfoot, Janet 15
Court Party 55, 62, 65, 67
Court of Session 69
Covenanters 15–16, 17, 18, 49
Cromartie, George Mackenzie, 1st Earl of 56
Cromwell, Oliver 54

Daiches, D. 65, 66
Darien Scheme 2, 23–9, 31, 48, 52, 55, 62–3, 71, 74, 104, 108–9
Defoe, Daniel 22, 41, 44, 51, 53, 94, 95
Devine, T. 36, 110

Disarming Acts 1716 and 1725 96
Douglas, Robert 25
Drummond, James 93

economy, Scottish 29, 30–2, 50–3, 75, 91–5, 102–3, 106, 109, 110
Edinburgh 44, 73, 93–4, 95, 111
empire 58, 102, 106, 107, 109, 110
English Act of Settlement 1701 33, 79
English Parliament 20–1, 29, 38
Enlightenment 111
Episcopalianism 19, 47, 56, 82, 96, 101
Equivalent, the (Article 15) 48, 62–3, 70, 71–2, 75, 101, 104
ethnic cleansing 14
exam preparation 114–34
  comparison questions 116, 122–6
  examples of answers 118–34
  'How far…?' questions 117, 126–30
  'How fully…?' questions 117, 130–4
  recall 117
  source evaluation questions 115–16, 118–21

famine 2, 30, 48
federal union 45, 67
Ferguson, N. 42, 107
Ferguson, W. 61, 63, 106
Fletcher of Saltoun, Andrew 31, 45–7, 64
France 32, 33, 51, 53, 79, 84, 87, 89
  war with 2, 4, 9, 40
Fraser of Lovat, Simon 35, 84–5
Fry, M. 107

Gaelic language 12, 96, 99
General Convention of the Royal Burghs 44

Index

gentry 57, 58
George I 79–80, 84
Glenlyon, Captain Robert Campbell of 9–11, 13, 14
Glenshiel, Battle of 1719 90–1
Glorious Revolution 1689 1–4, 5, 63
Godolphin, Earl of 69
Grant of Monymusk, Sir Archibald 103
Great Seal of Scotland 73, 76
Greenshields, James 101
Grierson, Sir Robert 18

Hamilton, James, 4th Duke of (Duke of Brandon) 48–9, 67, 101
Hamilton, William 102
Hanoverians 1, 33, 55, 70, 79–80
Haughs of Cromdale 9
Highland clans 5, 11–13, 81, 97
Highlands, effect of Union on 95–100
Hill, Colonel 11–12
Hodges, James 45
Hogarth, William 85
Honours of Scotland *see* Scottish crown jewels

Iain Lom (John MacDonald of Keppoch) 4, 11, 31
independence 46, 109
Ireland 9, 31, 54
Islay, Archibald Campbell, Earl of 95

Jacobite Rebellion 1689 4–9, 11, 31, 81
Jacobite Rebellion 1715 79–88
Jacobite Rebellion 1719 89–91
Jacobite Rebellion 1745–6 99
Jacobitism 4–9, 14, 19, 30, 49, 60, 63, 77, 79–91, 97, 106, 110
James VI of Scotland (James I of England) 20, 51
James VII of Scotland (James II of England) 3, 4, 7, 9, 11, 15, 16, 18, 19, 22, 32, 47, 56

James VIII of Scotland (James III of England) (James Francis Edward Stuart) 32, 79, 82, 86–7
Jardine, Allan 22
Jefferson, Thomas 46

Kidd, Captain William 21–2
Killiecrankie, Battle of 1689 6–9

Legislative War 1701–1705 32–9
Lenman, B. 5–6, 84
Leslie, Charles 14
Limerick, Treaty of 9
linen industry 94–5
'Little Ice Age' 30
Livingstone, Sir Thomas 12–13
Lockhart of Carnwath, George 60, 63, 67
Louis XIV 2, 3, 4, 29, 32
Louis XVI 84
Lynch, M. 91, 95, 103

MacDonalds 9–14, 31
MacIain, Chief of Glencoe MacDonalds 10, 11–12
Macinnes, A.I. 41, 55, 62, 67, 81, 85, 94, 95, 106, 109, 110
MacLeods 14, 99
Malt Tax 1725 92, 95
Mar, John Erskine, Earl of 80, 82, 83, 84, 86, 87, 102
Marchmont, Patrick Hume, Earl of 19, 47, 56
Marlborough, John Churchill, 1st Duke of 37, 38, 54
martyr 18
Mary (William and) 1–4, 56
Massacre of Glencoe 1692 2, 9–14, 29
mercantilism 20
Mitchison, R. 61
Monmouth Rebellion 47
Montrose, Earl of 62
MPs, Scottish 72, 74, 76, 104

National Covenant 1638 15
national identity, Scottish 44, 49, 70, 74, 104, 111

Navigation Acts 1660s and 1670s 20–1, 52, 108
Nicholson, Bishop William 83–4
Nine Years' War (1689–1697) 9, 29, 31
nobility 57–8, 72, 76

oath of allegiance 12–13
Old Pretender *see* James VIII of Scotland
Orange Lodge 2–3
Oswald, Roger 26, 27

Paterson, Bishop 15
Paterson, William 24, 25
Patronage Act 101
Paxman, J. 108
Peden, Alexander 16
peers, Scottish 72, 74, 76, 104
Pennecuik, Captain 26
Philip of Anjou 32
piracy 21–2
Pittenweem 15
Porteous Riot, Edinburgh 1736 93–4, 95
Presbyterianism 2, 15–19, 47, 53, 55, 82–3, 96, 100–1, 104, 106, 109
Preston, Battle of 1715 86
principles 55–6, 106, 109
privileges 70, 76, 109
Privy Council 3, 72, 101
protectionism 109
Protestantism 2, 3, 4, 15, 33, 47, 53, 84
see also Presbyterianism

Queensberry, James Douglas, 2nd Duke of 34–6, 64, 67, 69
'Queensberry Plot' (Scotch Plot) 1703 35

religion 15–19, 44, 47, 53, 55–6, 82–3, 104
Report of the Glencoe Enquiry 1695 12, 13
Riley, P. 106
Roxburgh, John Ker, 5th Earl of 54, 56–7, 62, 63

Index

salt tax 71, 95
Scots law 14, 70, 72, 76, 101, 104
Scott, P.H. 61, 106, 112
Scott, Sir Walter 16, 61, 76
Scottish Commissioners 48, 50, 51, 65, 67
Scottish Court of Exchequer 101
Scottish crown jewels 70, 74, 76
Scottish Estates 57
Scottish Parliament 2, 3–4, 19, 33, 34–6, 38, 42, 43, 45, 47–8, 49, 50, 55, 60, 67, 68–9, 108
Seafield, James Ogilvie, 1st Earl of 53, 69, 102
Seaforth, William MacKenzie, 5th Earl of 89–90
Selkirk, Alexander of Largo 22
Seton of Pitmedden 51–2, 65
Seymour, Sir Edward 40
Sharp, Archbishop 18
Shawfield Riot, Glasgow 92, 95
Sheriffmuir, Battle of 1715 80, 85–7
Sibbald, Sir Robert 30
Smout, T.C. 106
smuggling 75, 91–2, 94, 110
Society for Propagating Christian Knowledge 95–6
source analysis 114–34
sovereignty 33, 44, 49
Spain 24–5, 26–8, 32, 33, 89

Squadrone Volante 55–6, 62, 63, 67, 110
Stair, Sir John Dalrymple, Earl of 11, 12, 13, 24, 46
Starkey, David 111
Stevenson, Robert Louis 22
Stuarts 1, 6, 55, 79–80
succession 1–4, 32–3, 37, 53, 54, 70, 84, 104
superstition 93–4
Swift, Jonathan 41
Szechi, D. 80, 87

taxation 31, 44, 70, 71, 75, 80, 91–2, 94–5, 101, 104
Test Act 1681 15, 18
thumbscrews 15, 19
tobacco trade 102
Toleration Act 1712 101
Tories 75
torture 15, 19
trade
    domestic 31, 36, 38, 41, 44, 46, 50, 51, 66, 67, 70, 71, 101
    international 20–9, 34, 51, 58, 75, 102–3, 104, 107, 108–9
    see also black cattle trade
tramping 21
Treason, Law of 101
Treaty of Union 1707 see Union, Treaty of 1707
Tweeddale, John Hay, Earl of 36

Ulster 31
Union
    attempt to dissolve 1713 95, 102
    petitions against 44
Union, Treaty of 1707 35, 43, 50, 53, 55, 60–77, 106–13
    see also Articles of Union
United Provinces 2, 110
Utrecht, Treaty of 1713 84

Wade, General George 96
Wales 46
Walker, Patrick 30
War of the Spanish Succession 1701–1714 33, 34, 40, 41, 89
Whatley, C. 55, 56, 65, 67, 80, 106, 107
Whigs 55, 75, 84
Wigtown Martyrs 17–18
William of Orange 1–4, 11, 19, 22, 27–9, 33, 52, 56, 63, 79
Wilson, Margaret 17
Wine Act (Scottish) 1703 34, 108
witch-hunts 15, 31
Wolfe, James 42
Wool Act (Scottish) 1704 36, 108

Yule Vacance Act 101